# Animal-Assisted

## Interventions

## in Health Care Settings

A Best Practices Manual for Establishing New Programs

NEW DIRECTIONS IN THE HUMAN-ANIMAL BOND
Series editors Alan M. Beck and Marguerite E. O'Haire

# Animal-Assisted
## Interventions
## in Health Care Settings

**A Best Practices Manual for Establishing New Programs**

Sandra B. Barker, PhD

Rebecca A. Vokes

Randolph T. Barker, PhD

Purdue University Press / West Lafayette, Indiana

**Library of Congress Cataloging-in-Publication Data**

Names: Barker, Sandra B., 1950– author. | Vokes, Rebecca A., 1989–
author. | Barker, Randolph T. (Randolph Tinsley), 1951– author.

Title: Animal-assisted interventions in health care settings : a best
practices manual for establishing new programs / Sandra B. Barker,
Rebecca A. Vokes, Randolph T. Barker.

Other titles: New directions in the human-animal bond.

Description: West Lafayette, Indiana : Purdue University Press, [2019] |
Series: New directions in the human-animal bond | Includes bibliograph-
ical references.

Identifiers: LCCN 2018036881| ISBN 9781557538154 (pbk. : alk. paper) |
ISBN 9781612495378 (epdf) | ISBN 9781612495385 (epub)

Subjects: | MESH: Animal Assisted Therapy—organization & adminis-
tration | Health Services Administration | Program Development

Classification: LCC RM931.A65 | NLM WB 460 | DDC 615.8/5158—
dc23 LC record available at https://lccn.loc.gov/2018036881

**Cover images credit**

*Top left:* Lucy Stefani

*Top right:* Jordan Vance

*Bottom left:* monkeybusinessimages/iStock/Thinkstock

*Bottom right:* Will Gilbert

To access the complete manual, visit docs.lib.purdue.edu/AAI.

# Contents

# Preface

The way we conceptualize and deliver health care is changing rapidly. From the movement away from fee-for-service toward pay-for-performance, to the increasing weight assigned to patient satisfaction, health care organizations must find new paths to not only address patients' maladies, but enhance their overall well-being. It is in this environment that we look to complementary therapies: supplementing conventional clinical care, enhancing the patient experience, and improving the work environment for staff.

One such complementary therapy is animal-assisted interventions (AAI). Inquiries into the human–animal bond reveal new benefits applicable in the health care space, and with the availability of evidence-based guidelines, health care organizations enjoy a newfound flexibility to offer this service to patients, families, and staff.

At one large, urban, academic medical center, therapy dogs frequent the halls of the inpatient and outpatient units. As one medical resident said, "There is a dog in this hospital every day. We rely on them like we do any member of frontline staff."

Research from the field of human–animal interactions, extensive experience in health care administration, and lessons from years of program management in a comprehensive medical center inform this new model for effective, safe, and sustainable animal-assisted intervention programming. In addition to this comprehensive manual, an online template incorporating manual recommendations is available for download (docs.lib.purdue.edu/) AAI and easy tailoring to your specific facility.

It is important to note that this is not a training manual for AAI practitioners, as such manuals already exist and are referenced in our resource section. It is the hope of the authors that this manual will provide a basis for expansion of animal-assisted interventions spanning the vast array of health care delivery organizations serving needs across the care continuum. All proceeds from the sale of this manual will be donated to the Center for Human–Animal Interaction, a nonprofit 501(c)(3) organization in the Virginia Commonwealth University School of Medicine, Richmond, Virginia, USA.

Thank you to the members of the Society for Healthcare Epidemiology of America (SHEA) Guidelines Committee who reviewed this manual's recommendations related to infection prevention and control.

# 1

# The Health Care Administrator's Overview of AAI

Health care administrators face numerous challenges as they seek to provide the best experience and value for patients, as well as a fulfilling and healthy work environment for their teams. Evaluations of health care facilities once hinged on patient outcomes. However, in the age of pay-for-performance, reimbursements are increasingly based on quality, value, and patient experience. Additionally, health care administrators must recruit and retain a strong health care workforce while managing dissatisfaction and burnout among providers.

Evidence-based medicine supports provision of safe and effective clinical care, and now a new field of research seeks to provide evidence-based complementary therapy, improving patient experience, addressing provider stress, and adding value across the health care continuum. This manual was developed to provide guidance for health care administrators, managers, volunteer coordinators, and their staffs in establishing and coordinating one such complementary therapy, animal-assisted interventions (AAI), in health care facilities.

The manual reflects over a decade of direct experience in coordinating and maintaining an animal-assisted therapy (AAT), animal-assisted activity (AAA), and facility animal program in a major academic medical center; conducting research demonstrating the program's effectiveness and contributing to the evidence base on the health benefits of animal-assisted interventions; and providing education and consultation on AAI in health care facilities. In addition, current resources relevant to AAI in health care settings were consulted and are listed in Additional Resources.

The recommendations presented are intended to offer program structure, best practices, and guidelines for AAI program evaluation as well as establish policies that maximize patient, staff, and AAI team safety and minimize risk. Since it is not feasible for this manual to cover all types of health care facilities, recommendations are offered for the most restrictive settings, acute care hospitals, with the understanding that these recommendations can be extended to other facilities such as residential and outpatient facilities. Administrators in less acute health care settings may wish to tailor these recommendations based on their specific needs.

Because dogs are the only species recommended for AAI in acute health care settings (Murthy et al., 2015), this manual refers specifically to therapy dogs and their human handlers, referred to throughout as "AAI teams."

## 1.1 Benefits of AAI

Published studies investigating the potential impact of AAI in health care facilities provide evidence of a number of benefits.

However, it is important to point out that not all studies find patient benefits, which may be due to the type of intervention implemented, client population selected, and study design. Most interventions studied are structured or unstructured animal-assisted activities, rather than animal-assisted therapy in which the animals are an active component in a patient's care plan. The vast majority of AAI studied have been conducted with therapy dogs.

Several studies report benefits for cardiovascular patients, including patients with congestive heart failure (Abate, Zucconi, & Boxer, 2011; Cole, Gawlinski, Steers, & Kotlerman, 2007), with hypertension (Allen, Shykoff, & Izzo, 2001), and post–myocardial infarction (Friedmann, Thomas, & Son, 2011). Published studies also show benefits for orthopedic patients post–joint replacement surgery (Havey, Vlasses, Vlasses, Ludwig-Beymer, & Hackbarth, 2014), as well as for women hospitalized with high-risk pregnancies (Lynch et al., 2014). Studies of AAI with psychiatric patients (Bardill & Hutchinson, 1997; Barker & Dawson, 1998; Nepps, Stewart, & Bruckno, 2014) also report benefits. While some evidence supports benefits for hospitalized children (Calcaterra et al., 2015; Kaminski, Pellino, & Wish, 2002; Sobo, Eng, & Kassity-Krich, 2006; Tsai, Friedmann, & Thomas, 2010), a recent critical review of the literature on AAI in pediatric hospitals cautions about the lack of sound evidence and calls for more rigorous research with this population (Chur-Hansen, McArthur, Winefield, Hanieh, & Hazel, 2014).

AAI has also been found to benefit health care staff. Health care professionals interacting with therapy dogs in an acute care hospital were reported to have reduced stress after these interactions, evidenced from reduced serum and salivary cortisol levels after very brief time spent with a therapy dog (Barker, Knisely, McCain, & Best, 2005).

Finally, AAI has been shown to improve patient perceptions of treatment in a health care facility. A recent study in orthopedic surgery patients found that inclusion of therapy dog visitation resulted in improved scoring in top box Hospital Consumer Assessment of Healthcare Providers and Systems measures including nurse communication, pain management, and overall hospital rating (Harper et al., 2015). Another study found that AAI with a therapy dog produced significant reduction in self-reported anxiety scores of adolescent gynecology patients in an outpatient setting (McCracken, LaJoie, Polis, Hertweck, & Loveless, 2016).

While more rigorous research is needed to confirm preliminary studies documenting benefits of AAI for health care patients (and staff), there is a growing body of evidence supporting AAI as a low-cost, complementary therapy with the potential to benefit many patients. Regardless of the evidence supporting AAI, a major barrier to implementing AAI in health care facilities is negative beliefs and fears about dogs in such facilities. Four of the common myths about AAI are addressed in the following section.

## 1.2 Myths About AAI

There are several widespread myths related to AAI, all of which can be addressed by having appropriate policies and procedures in place. Four of the more common myths are discussed below.

### Therapy Dogs Will Spread Infections

With appropriate policies and procedures in place, the risk of zoonotic disease transmission is quite low, with dogs posing the lowest risk (Murthy et al., 2015). Health care facilities with successful AAI programs have strict requirements for therapy animals and their handlers, including appropriate species for their settings, registration, health, temperament, and cleanliness policies along with strict procedures for visitation.

### Therapy Dogs Will Be Dirty and Bring Ticks and Fleas Into the Facility

Appropriate policies that address cleanliness ensure that therapy animals are well groomed and recently bathed, most within 24 hours of a visit. Policies that require therapy animals to be on flea and tick prevention programs and that have designated exercise areas for therapy animals minimize the risk of ticks and fleas being introduced to the facility by AAI programs. It is also important to be aware that patients, visitors, staff, and volunteers often have pets at home and may bring fleas and ticks into the facility on their clothes and belongings.

### Therapy Dogs Will Be Disruptive—Bark and Jump on People

AAI program policies requiring appropriate training of therapy dogs minimize the chances of disruptive behavior and address any disruptive behavior that may occur. While dogs may occasionally bark in a facility, appropriately trained handlers quickly stop any barking or other potentially disruptive behavior.

### Therapy Dogs Will Negatively Impact Productivity and Patient Care

There is no evidence to support the myth that therapy dogs will interfere with productivity and patient care. To the contrary, health care professionals have been found to experience reduced physiological stress after very brief interactions with therapy dogs. In our own experience providing AAI to hospital staff at highly stressful times, we receive consistent positive feedback on the ability of therapy dogs to calm and comfort staff. Appropriately trained therapy dog teams and carefully developed policies and procedures for patient interactions minimize the possibility of any interference in patient care and maximize the potential of

AAI playing a complementary role in patient care. Policies and procedures addressing these types of issues will be presented later in this manual.

## 1.3 Limiting Therapy Animals in Acute Health Care Facilities to Dogs

Many species of animals are used in AAI including dogs, horses, cats, birds, alpacas, guinea pigs, and rabbits. Some species may visit at a facility with their handler, and some species must be visited and interacted with at the facility where they are housed. For example, while a therapy dog might be brought by her handler into a physical rehabilitation center to visit with patients, patients might visit an equine therapy center in order to visit and partake in therapeutic horseback riding. All animals (with the exception of fish) pose a risk due to the potential for injury from contact with teeth (accidental or intentional), injury from scratch (accidental or intentional), or general abrasion or bruise from contact.

The Centers for Disease Control and Prevention (2017) defines zoonotic diseases as diseases caused by viruses, bacteria, parasites, and fungi that can be spread between animals and humans. All animals pose the risk of zoonotic disease transmission to humans.

Cats may be appropriate for use in AAI in some settings, but are not appropriate for visitation in an acute health care environment due to their less reliable nature and higher risk of zoonotic disease transmission due to risk of scratching with claws (intentional or accidental). Other animals (such as horses) that primarily live in an outdoor setting are not appropriate for an acute health care setting due to their common contact with contaminant sources common to the outdoors.

It is recommended that exclusively dogs be used in a health care facility, and particularly in an acute care setting. Dogs are easily trainable, have generally predictable behavior, are familiar to most individuals as an accepted animal for therapy and service, and generally enjoy human contact. Dogs can be used widely in any setting (acute care, ambulatory care, home health), and also have wide variation in size (some dogs are small enough to be placed on a patient's lap, while other dogs are large enough to stand adjacent to a patient's bed or wheelchair). Finally, dogs carry relatively few communicable diseases.

## 1.4 Key Definitions

Health care administrators should have an understanding of basic terminology used in AAI in order to accurately communicate the purpose and activities involved in their AAI programming. Additionally, these definitions should be clearly explained to all AAI teams (see Chapter 5, Section 5.4: Manuals for AAI Teams).

### *Animal-Assisted Intervention (AAI)*
AAI is an encompassing term describing the use of an animal in a capacity beneficial to humans (American Veterinary Medicine Association, 2018). AAI is conducted in many settings, typically using therapy animals. Therapy animals may include any species appropriate to the target setting. AAI in health care settings usually involves therapy animals working with a human handler to provide animal-assisted therapy (AAT) and/or animal-assisted activities (AAA).

### *Animal-Assisted Therapy (AAT)*
AAT is the purposeful incorporation of a therapy animal into an individual's treatment plan. AAT may include a health care professional involving a therapy animal while working with a patient to achieve a treatment goal (such as brushing a dog to improve

eye-hand coordination). Patient responses to AAT are typically documented in the medical record by health care professionals.

### Animal-Assisted Activities (AAA)

AAA are less structured than AAT, but evidence suggests they are also beneficial for patients, families, and staff. The goals of AAA may include relaxation, fun, and distraction from pain or discomfort. AAA are not considered part of a formal treatment plan, and thus do not require documentation in the medical record by the professionals caring for the patient. Please note that most therapy animal interactions in acute health care settings consist of patient visitation and are categorized as AAA.

### Service Animals

Service animals are defined and protected in the United States under the Americans with Disabilities Act of 1990 (ADA). Service animals are individually trained to perform specific tasks for people with disabilities. Examples of such work or tasks include guiding people who are blind, alerting people who are deaf, pulling a wheelchair, alerting and protecting a person who is having a seizure, or reminding a person with mental illness to take prescribed medications. The only two species defined as service animals under ADA are dogs and miniature horses (horses measuring 24–34 inches to the shoulder, and weighing 70–100 pounds). The following are additional important points regarding service animals:

1. Service animals are working animals, not pets.
2. The work or task a service animal has been trained to provide must be directly related to the person's disability.
3. A person with a disability has a legal right to enter public places with his or her service animal, including banks, restaurants, stores, and other public venues.

4. Service animals typically perform specific tasks for their owners and are not to engage with those around them.
5. Service animals must be under control and leashed unless the leash interferes with the animal's tasks.

For more information about service animals, please see the Americans with Disabilities Act of 1990 under the U.S. Department of Justice, Civil Rights Division, Disability Rights Section.

### Therapy Animals

Therapy animals meet health, behavior, and temperament criteria for appropriateness to participate in AAI. A wide variety of animal species may be considered therapy animals. Therapy animals do not have the same legal standing as service animals and are not covered by the Americans with Disabilities Act of 1990. They do not have legal access to public and/or private areas and must receive administrative permission to visit in any facility.

### Emotional Support Animals

An emotional support animal is a companion animal that provides therapeutic benefit to an individual with a mental or health-related disability (American Veterinary Medicine Association, 2018). These support animals may provide companionship, relieve loneliness, and sometimes help with depression, anxiety, and certain phobias, but do not have special training to perform tasks that assist people with disabilities. Emotional support animals do not have the same legal standing as service dogs and are not covered by the Americans with Disabilities Act of 1990. Emotional support animals are provided legal protection in the United States under the Fair Housing Act of 1968, Section 504, which states that individuals with a disability may request reasonable accommodation for their emotional support dog. Emotional support animals are also provided legal protection by the

Department of Transportation, which requires U.S. airlines to provide transport for emotional support animals when persons with mental health-related disabilities require their emotional support animal be present in order to travel.

For more information regarding regulations related to emotional support animals under the U.S. Department of Transportation please see the Air Carrier Access Act (ACAA) or visit www .transportation.gov.

For more information regarding regulations related to emotional support animals under the U.S. Department of Housing and Urban Development, please visit www.hud.gov.

## 1.5 Zoonotic Diseases and Prevention

While AAI is considered safe in acute health care settings due to availability of evidence-based infection prevention techniques (Murthy et al., 2015), it is essential for administrators to know the risks associated with therapy dog visitation in acute health care settings, and to involve hospital personnel responsible for infection prevention in AAI program planning. The following zoonotic diseases are associated with dogs (Centers for Disease Control and Prevention, 2017):

- *Ancylostoma brazilense, A. caninum, A. ceylanicum, Unicinaria stenocephala* (Hookworm)
- Brucellosis (bacterial infection causing flu-like symptoms; may sometimes develop into a chronic and difficult to treat condition)
- *Campylobacter* (gastrointestinal bacteria causing abdominal cramping, diarrhea, and fever)
- *Capnocytophaga* (bacterial infection that is generally not problematic in healthy humans, but may result in complications in patients with compromised immune systems)

- Cryptosporidiosis (parasitic disease causing severe diarrhea and vomiting; may cause complications in humans with compromised immune systems)
- *Dipylidium caninum* (Ringworm)
- Echinococcosis (parasitic disease that can result in tapeworms growing on different organs of the body, including the lungs and liver)
- Ehrlichiosis (bacterial disease resulting in possible fever, headache, chills, muscle pain, nausea, vomiting, diarrhea, and rash)
- Giardiasis (parasite causing gastrointestinal issues including diarrhea, abdominal cramps, nausea, and vomiting)
- Leishmaniasis (protozoan causing painful ulcers on the skin; visceral leishmaniasis is less common and is characterized by fever, weight loss, enlarged spleen, and anemia)
- Leptospirosis (bacterial disease that often results in no symptoms for humans, although some may have nonspecific flu-like signs; can result in more serious disease)
- Lyme disease (bacterial disease causing flu-like symptoms; may also result in symptoms such as arthritis and loss of facial muscle tone, and can be fatal)
- Pasteurellosis (bacterial disease that can cause painful wound and skin infections, in severe cases widespread infection, and might affect the nervous system)
- Plague (symptoms include sudden onset of high fever, chills, headache, malaise, and swollen lymph nodes; forms include septicemic, pneumonic, and bubonic)
- Rabies (a viral neurological disease fatal in humans and animals if untreated)
- Rocky Mountain spotted fever (symptoms may include fever, rash, headache, nausea, vomiting, abdominal pain, and muscle pain)
- Salmonellosis (infection causing diarrhea, vomiting, fever, or abdominal cramps)

- Sarcoptic mange (parasitic skin disease that will not infect humans, but may result in bites from the mites that cause the disease)
- Methicillin-resistant *Staphylococcus aureus* (MRSA bacteria causing skin infections that can range from mild to severe; if left untreated, MRSA can spread to the bloodstream or lungs and cause life-threatening infections)
- *Toxocara* (Roundworm)

Many diseases may be prevented with proper vaccination (e.g., rabies), and the risk of transfer of a communicable disease from a dog to an individual in a health care facility can be minimized through proper interaction and procedures that emphasize infection control (see Figure 1). This means that both volunteer AAI teams and frontline staff should be prepared to execute and communicate proper procedures with therapy animals. Administrators

**Figure 1** A therapy dog relaxes on a patient bed while lying on a sheet, which acts as a barrier between the underside of the dog and the patient's linens. Use of cloth barriers is one infection prevention method used in AAI. (Photo by Matt Stanton.)

should work directly with hospital infection prevention personnel, unit managers, volunteer managers, and any other team members who are responsible for communication of proper infection control procedures to volunteers and staff.

# 2

# AAI Program Structure

Similar to clinical and support services, complementary therapies should be structured based on the market a health care facility serves. Health care administrators should consider the mission, vision, and values that govern their organization, and determine how the AAI program may support the overall strategy of the organization. For example, if a health care organization distinguishes itself in areas such as physician satisfaction, AAI may be targeted to providers as well as their patients. Health care administrators must determine who is responsible for the service, which populations to serve, and how the service will be financed. In this chapter we will examine key considerations in structuring animal-assisted intervention (AAI) programming.

## 2.1 Target Population

The *target population* refers to the group of individuals that the AAI program seeks to serve. Identifying the AAI program's target population will influence program structure, policies and procedures, and activities, so it is important to define the target population from the beginning in the development of the AAI program. Your target population may include pediatric, adult, geriatric, psychiatric, military veterans, and/or your own employees. You should determine the setting where your target population seeks care such as inpatient units, outpatient clinics, or even in their own homes. Patient volume and population census data may be used to estimate the number of patients your program wishes to serve. These estimates (along with frequency of visitation discussed in this chapter under 2.4: Defining the Intervention) will determine how many AAI teams are needed to provide services, and will also inform program administrators in making decisions on staffing as well as possibly expanding to other populations and facilities. For instance, if needs are being adequately addressed for your target population, the program may consider expansion to another facility or target population.

## 2.2 Special Populations

Within your health care environment, there may be populations with differing needs and characteristics. Below are six special populations an AAI program may serve, and some specific considerations for each population. Please note that policies and suggested interactions for all patients can be clearly communicated to AAI teams in a manual (see Chapter 5, Section 5.4: Manuals for AAI Teams) and are included in the downloadable manual template (docs.lib.purdue.edu/AAI).

### Pediatric Patients
Pediatric settings can be complex and dynamic, and many factors should be considered in developing an AAI program for pediatric patients. Consultation with a child life specialist or other

**Figure 2** This therapy dog reacts to a child's touch by closing her eyes and relaxing her mouth. Her body language indicates she is comfortable visiting with this pediatric patient. (Photo by Jordan Vance.)

designated professional is essential on a pediatric unit, as different sets of familial and social circumstances may be involved in the care of each pediatric patient. Pediatric units are highly stimulating for dogs, and additional temperament and training requirements are advised to ensure all therapy dogs participating on pediatric units are comfortable and appropriate in such environments (see Figure 2).

Similarly, not all therapy dog owner/handlers will be comfortable visiting very sick children or those with terminal illnesses. AAI programs should ensure that the child life specialist or other designated liaison is involved in approving, orienting, and providing support for each AAI team that serves on the unit. While one orientation may prepare AAI teams to visit with a general patient population at a health care facility, an additional orientation should take place on the pediatrics unit with a designated pediatric liaison in order to familiarize the AAI team with the unique environment and expectations in pediatrics.

Pediatric patients may differ from other populations in how they interact with AAI teams. First, it should be noted that children at different ages vary in their physical and cognitive stages of development, and therefore may react differently to therapy dogs than adult patients. For example, while normal dog behavior like sniffing a person's hand may be perfectly acceptable to an adult or an older child, a young child may find this proximity to an animal's face and mouth alarming. A child may cry or have a similar outburst unexpectedly, or a child might have difficulty petting and handling an animal appropriately. Additionally, a four-year-old child may have limited control over the force with which she pets a dog on the head, or the strength of her embrace, and pet a dog very roughly. AAI teams should be adequately prepared for these types of common behaviors while serving in a pediatrics unit, and dogs should be temperament tested with simulated circumstances commonly found in pediatric settings in order to safely interact with young children. Appraisal of a dog's comfort interacting with pediatric patients should be conducted by an appropriate AAI staff member. An AAI program should consider conducting recurrent reviews of a therapy dog's temperament in order to continue service on a pediatric unit, as a dog's tolerance may change with age.

Pediatric patients also may be limited in their ability to verbalize important information about their conditions. This can lead to circumstances that put patients at risk. For example, if a child is lying in a bed and is covered by sheets, the AAI team may not know that they have an injured leg. The child may not be able to tell them, or understand information about their condition that is important to relay to an AAI team. It is therefore vital that AAI teams communicate with adults responsible for a pediatric patient and the health care team before any interactions.

Hand sanitation by anyone interacting with the dog, both before and after the interaction, is mandatory. This includes the dog handler. If sanitizer is used on a child's hands, there is a risk that it may be ingested if the child is not properly supervised. Hand sanitation procedures should be discussed with a child life specialist in advance of interactions as well. It may be advisable to leave sanitation procedures pre- and postvisit at the discretion of the guardian or care team member present with the child. Again, it is important to keep communication open between child life specialists or designated pediatric liaisons, AAI program staff, and AAI teams in order to maintain the safety and enjoyment of AAI for pediatric patients and their families.

### Geriatric Patients

Geriatric patients with a variety of medical needs can make up a large portion of the overall patient population in a health care facility. It is important for AAI programs to educate their teams to appropriately serve geriatric patients in these facilities.

First, sensory perception may be limited for a geriatric patient, and an AAI team must make sure that the patient has agreed to a visit before interacting. For example, if the geriatric patient is an inpatient on a psychiatric unit, it is important that a designated staff member from that unit serves as a liaison for the AAI team and obtains consent for the visit from the patient. If a geriatric patient is experiencing sensory limitations (for example, partial hearing loss), it may be sufficient for an AAI team to simply take extra care announcing the team's presence on the unit.

Second, when interacting with a geriatric patient, special care must be taken to prevent accident or injury from falls due to changes in balance, motor skills, and perception. Interacting with a therapy dog should be carefully monitored, with special attention paid to the position of the dog, position of harnesses and leash, and any other tripping hazards in the immediate environment. AAI program staff may choose to work with the staff on a unit in order to ensure that a safe area (with ample room to maneuver the therapy dog and area for patients to be seated) is available for interaction with geriatric patients. When a geriatric patient is less mobile, a visit to the patient's bedside may be preferable. In this instance, AAI program procedures need to include guidelines regarding any weight or size limitations for dogs permitted onto beds to lie with patients. It is advisable to include handler recommendations for dogs to sit or lie down while interacting with an ambulatory geriatric patient. As with anyone interacting with a dog, hand sanitation procedures must be followed before and after contact with the therapy dog.

Third, geriatric patients may also have limited dexterity, making petting either difficult or potentially less comfortable for the animal. Therefore, it is important for AAI program guidelines to remind handlers to carefully monitor their dogs for any signs of stress or discomfort, removing them from the interaction if these signs are shown.

### Pregnant Patients

Many patients who are pregnant will be encountered on labor and delivery units, and while some facilities may choose to prohibit visitation, AAI can be of value to these patients. As with all areas receiving AAI, consulting with staff of the labor and delivery unit should take place prior to AAI visitation.

When interacting with pregnant patients, the health and safety of the mother and her unborn child must be considered. Pregnant women, particularly those in the third trimester, may be at increased risk for a fall. AAI program guidelines must educate handlers about these risks and the need to carefully monitor therapy dog interactions with these patients, with special attention paid to the position of the dog, position of harness and leash, and any other tripping hazards in the immediate environment. Therefore it may be advisable for handlers to instruct their dogs to sit or lie down while interacting with pregnant patients. It is also important to carefully observe hand sanitation practices before and after contact with AAI team, as any infection could prove dangerous to both mother and unborn child.

### Patients With Psychiatric Disorders

Psychiatric patients have been found to benefit greatly from AAI, and it is important to provide access to AAI while maintaining the comfort and safety of volunteers, patients, and unit staff. AAI can be structured in a one-on-one visitation, or in a group setting that may encourage participation and social support. AAI program staff should consult with staff on the inpatient psychiatric unit to determine the most effective and safe procedures for patients and staff. Program staff should also identify at least one staff member willing to serve as a liaison for AAI teams when they are present on the unit.

Psychiatric disorders range in presentation and in severity, and special sensitivity and care must be used by any volunteer in an inpatient psychiatric setting. AAI teams visiting acute psychiatric services will benefit from an orientation to psychiatric patients to prepare them for visiting the type of patients treated in the setting; that is, patients who may be experiencing hallucinations, delusions, cognitive decline, and/or impulsivity. All AAI teams should be accompanied by an appropriate liaison (for example, a psychiatric nurse or social worker) who can screen psychiatric patients for appropriateness for AAI). On some units, security measures must be taken for the safety of patients and staff and these extend to the AAI team. These measures may include security checkpoints and panic or alert buttons carried by the AAI team while visiting on an inpatient psychiatric unit. As with all patients, hand sanitation must be performed before and after contact with the AAI team. If psychiatric patients are unable or have difficulty sanitizing their own hands, the handler may aid them in using the hand sanitizer, or may turn to the staff liaison accompanying them to ask for assistance sanitizing the hands of patients.

### Secure Care Patients

Secure care units (SCU) treat patients who are incarcerated and present an alternative to a prison hospital unit. These patients often have received no visitors for an extended period of time and welcome the opportunity to interact with a therapy dog. It is important for AAI programs to set guidelines that prioritize the safety of patients, staff, and volunteers by working closely with SCU staff and security professionals assigned to the unit. SCUs often operate under a collaborative agreement between state corrections departments and the hospital and will have officers present at all times. The appropriate administrative personnel should be consulted and involved when initiating AAI for SCU patients.

Rules for interacting with patients on this unit should be clear and well known to any visiting AAI team. AAI teams may be asked to stow personal belongings elsewhere before visiting in an SCU. Cell phones are generally prohibited as these patients are prohibited from accessing telephones. Patients in the SCU should be encouraged by the handler to use hand sanitizer before and after visiting with the therapy dog. If an SCU patient is unable or has difficulty sanitizing their own hands, the handler may aid them in using the hand sanitizer, or may turn to SCU staff for assistance sanitizing the hands of the patient.

### Other Special Patient Populations

If other special populations are included in your target population for AAI program services, policies and procedures will need to address any unique needs of these populations. Consulting with a designated liaison for the special population (child life specialist for pediatric patients, nurse or social worker for psychiatric patients) in creating these specific policies and procedures is advisable. Additional orientations and training of AAI teams may be required for safe interaction with special populations and for the comfort of the AAI teams. While sanitation should always take place before and after contact with a therapy dog, practices may need to be adjusted in consideration of each patient populations' potential cognitive or physical state.

## 2.3 Space

While a dedicated physical presence in the facility served by the AAI program is preferable, available space in health care facilities is often limited and the sharing of existing administrative space may need to be arranged to provide an appropriate location for oversight of the program. At a minimum, adequate administrative space is needed to store AAI team records (documentation of therapy dog registration, completion of facility volunteer requirements, annual animal health screening, etc.), team identification apparel (volunteer shirts, dog vests, leashes, etc.), as well as informational program materials (procedural manual, brochures, etc.). Computer access is needed for electronic communication, database management, and record storage.

Ideally, AAI programs will be housed in their own separate room(s). A shared workspace for program staff with separate desks for each staff member allows for collaboration and independent work. A separate office for the program director or coordinator allows for discretion and privacy when appropriate. Two additional considerations for space include access to a conference room to allow for larger group meetings and educational/informational presentations, and separate storage space to house materials necessary for the operations of the AAI program.

AAI services may be provided in individual patient rooms, group activity rooms, and/or common areas depending on the facility and target population. Designated outdoor space in close proximity to the health care facility must be identified for exercising dogs and for sanitary elimination away from patient areas. Designated areas for AAI team parking may be needed, depending on the facility.

## 2.4 Defining the Intervention

Once the target population and space requirements have been defined, consideration of the type of AAI (group or individual) most appropriate for the facility should be addressed. Some health care facilities benefit most from AAI at designated times by small groups of AAI teams. Such group visits typically take place with interested patients brought to a large common room and are monitored by staff. The activity may take place with several AAI teams present at once, or one AAI team visiting all of the patients in the group. This type of group activity may work well in a lower acuity setting such as a partial hospitalization program or a skilled nursing facility. This type of group AAI may also support the goals of treatment in ways that private visitation would not. For example, a psychiatrist may ask an AAI team to be present prior (or during if the therapy dog handler happens to be employed on psychiatry services) to group therapy sessions in order to encourage attendance by patients on an inpatient psychiatric unit and increase interaction among patients.

Other facilities may choose to structure AAI individually with one AAI team visiting one patient room at a time. The latter option allows for more personalized interactions with the AAI team for patients, families, and staff, but requires more planning and AAI team orientation and preparation. Additional aid from staff in the form of escorts may be needed for individual visitation in some areas, or AAI teams may need additional materials such as linens, sanitizers, maps, and unit guides in order to safely visit if unaccompanied by staff. Generally, individual visitation is preferable in acute inpatient settings, not only to reach more patients, but also to minimize risk of cross contamination between patients in group settings. Additionally, there is less risk of inappropriate interactions or distractions between dogs when AAI teams visit alone as opposed to as a group.

## 2.5 AAI Program Staffing

Staffing for an AAI program varies according to the program size, structure of interventions, and the resources available in the community and facility. Administrators should consult with human resources team members in order to determine appropriate design, recruitment, and onboarding for any positions associated with the AAI program. Additionally, the U.S. Office of Personnel Management and the U.S. Department of Labor provide online resources for job analysis, job design, and employee assessment and selection (please see Additional Resources). Ideally, a dedicated administrative staff person (program director/administrator) with a background in AAI practice, program administration skills, and expertise in coordinating volunteers is hired to direct the program. This individual works closely with the volunteer office of the health care facility, and should report to appropriate health care administrators (see Figure 3). Other staff members may be external or internal hires, internal transfers, or employees who may benefit from job redesign.

Most AAI programs in health care facilities deliver services by recruiting either an existing AAI group in the community or individual volunteers with dogs meeting requirements of the AAI program. AAI teams are typically not employees of the health care facility. However, employees of some health care facilities have developed programs in which health care professionals train their own dogs to meet the AAI requirements of the facility, including the approved therapy dog registration organizations, in which they provide professional services. These professionals may then incorporate their therapy dog into the treatment of their clients.

Since most AAI programs involve community volunteers, a dedicated AAI program director in the health care facility is essential to coordinate and maintain oversight of the program (see Figure 3). Additional staff may be needed as the program grows.

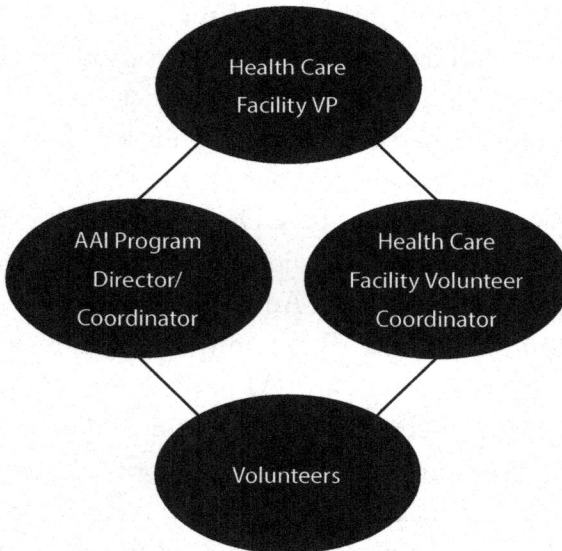

**Figure 3** Sample basic AAI program organizational chart. The AAI coordinator/director should have a clear reporting line to a hospital administrator and maintain regular communication with the volunteer coordinator of the facility. In this instance, AAI teams at the facility have dual reporting to both the AAI program leader and the volunteer manager.

## 2.6 AAI Program Operational Tasks

Certain tasks may be considered essential and integral to the program operation. These tasks may include

- ongoing strategic and operational planning;
- developing, monitoring, and revising AAI program policy and procedures;
- recruiting AAI teams;
- educating and training AAI teams;
- monitoring dog and human handler compliance with health care facility and AAI program requirements;
- developing and maintaining records of AAI team presence in the health care facility and patients and staff receiving AAI services;
- maintaining communication with AAI teams;
- collaborating with key health care facility staff in AAI service area;
- fundraising for program needs; and
- educating internal and external groups about the AAI program.

The following tasks may be added as personnel and resources increase:

- conducting periodic evaluation and research activities to develop an evidence base for the program;
- educating others inside and outside of the health care facility on the benefits of AAI through lectures, invited presentations, and development and dissemination of educational materials; and
- developing community partnerships and sponsorship.

As programs increase in size and scope, so do the resource demands. Funding additional program staff, such as a volunteer coordinator, may be needed to assist the program director as AAI teams and services grow. Successful AAI programs involve inter-disciplinary collaboration for the development, approval, imple-mentation, and maintenance of the program. Employees of a health care facility who may be involved (see Figure 4) to varying degrees with the program may include

- administrators;
- chaplains;
- mental health professionals;
- nurses;
- occupational, physical, and recreational therapists;
- physicians;
- quality and safety personnel; and
- volunteer coordinators.

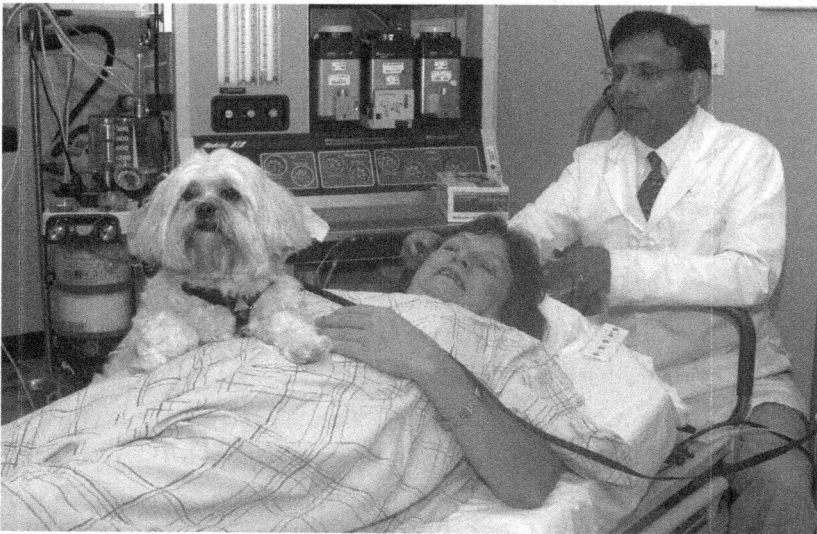

**Figure 4** A psychiatrist prepares a patient for electroconvulsive therapy (ECT) with a therapy dog present. A wide variety of practitioners incorporate AAI in their practice to improve the patient experience. (Photo by Jim Mattson.)

In addition to employees, students may intern or volunteer for the program. Community members not participating as AAI teams may also volunteer to assist with AAI program activities.

## 2.7 Funding

Adequate funding is vital for the implementation and maintenance of AAI programs. Funding is necessary for a variety of basic operations including the recruitment of new AAI teams, provision of some type of team identification, maintenance of AAI team records, coordination of visits in the facility, oversight and review of AAI teams, and evaluation of the program.

Ideally, funding is provided by the facility receiving AAI services. Additional resources may be sought in the form of grants, donations, endowments, and fundraising activities in the health care facility and the surrounding community. While donations of both goods and capital can be actively sought from external sources, the AAI program should have some degree of continuing and dedicated support from the system in which it operates. This could include a program cost center from which to purchase office items, shared space for offices or program administration, and/or personnel costs.

In the United States, an AAI program may qualify for tax exempt status under the IRS Tax Code section 501(c)(3). With this qualification, the AAI program will be eligible to receive tax-deductible contributions under Code section 170 (www.irs. gov). It should also be noted that some AAI program activities may constitute a community benefit under the IRS Form 990 Schedule H. Administrators should consult with finance personnel in order to determine the appropriate designation of any particular AAI program.

# 3

# Establishing Requirements:
# AAI Program Entry

Health care facilities should have clear policies to address all animals permitted in the facility. This may include therapy dogs, service animals, and facility dogs, where appropriate. Formal policies and procedures specifically for AAI and safety should be developed in collaboration with different departments and/or staff members with a stake or interest in the program, such as volunteer services, infection control, physicians, administrators, and nursing services. Therapy dogs should not be permitted to enter the health care facility without being enrolled in your AAI program. Please note that the recommendations in this chapter are included in the online downloadable template (docs .lib.purdue.edu/AAI) administrators can tailor to their facility.

AAI policies should address

- the purpose of the AAI program;
- dog and handler requirements for participating in the AAI program, including training, registration, renewal, retraining and reinstatement, and retirement; and
- AAI procedures, including areas approved for visitation, maximizing patient safety, proper sanitation, dog welfare, therapy dog identification, and handling adverse events.

For maximizing patient, staff, and AAI team safety, several basic policies and procedures are advised to supplement health care facility's existing policies and procedures:

- AAI teams must be registered and currently enrolled in your facility's AAI program to enter the health care facility.
- AAI teams will only visit patients in approved areas and not have contact with patients allergic to dogs or in isolation.
- AAI teams must adhere to all program policies and procedures set forth by the AAI program and health care facility or be excluded from participation.
- AAI teams must meet all health care facility requirements for volunteers.
- AAI teams may visit no longer than two hours per day with a break after one hour.

## 3.1 Therapy Dog Evaluation and Testing

It is critical to require that appropriate evaluation and testing of any dog entering a health care facility take place before engaging in AAI. Evaluation of fitness and health of the dog, evaluation of the dog's temperament, and testing of all control commands (e.g., sit, stay, come) should be completed. Relying on a reputable, external therapy animal organization to test and evaluate dogs for work in your health care facility provides external validation of a dog's appropriateness for participating in AAI. However, these organizations vary in the rigor and comprehensiveness of their evaluation criteria. This chapter addresses the important evaluation criteria to consider in selecting an external therapy dog registration organization for an acute health care facility. Links to several external organizations that evaluate and register therapy dogs are provided in Additional Resources.

The registration group(s) that you select to meet initial requirements for participation in your AAI program should evaluate dogs and their handlers for appropriateness in health care facilities and emphasize behaviors to maximize safety of patients and staff. The evaluation must include screening for any sign of aggression by a dog as an indication that the dog is not appropriate for therapy dog work. Basic therapy dog control commands that registration organizations require are depicted in Table 1.

For all health care settings, it is important for therapy dog evaluations to include the dog's proper response to control commands in crowded areas, and with distractions such as food (see "Leave It," Table 1). For everyone's safety, the dog must consistently walk on a leash without pulling, walk on a leash through a crowd, and walk past other dogs and people without pulling on the leash. These control commands ensure that the dog is able to maneuver through the environment while avoiding potential hazards, and minimizing the chance of injury to patients, family, staff, and visitors in the facility. Control commands also ensure that in an emergency situation, handlers can maintain control over their dogs safely and effectively.

Temperament testing is an important measure of a dog's appropriateness for participation in AAI. Situations specific to your health care facility should be tested. For example, a dog must

**TABLE 1** *Illustration of Basic Control Commands for AAI Teams*

| Command | Command Description | Example Image of Command |
|---------|---------------------|--------------------------|
| "Sit" | Dog is instructed to place hindquarters on the floor. | |
| "Stay" | Dog is instructed to remain stationary until released. | |
| "Down" | Dog is instructed to lie down on the floor. | |

**TABLE 1** *Illustration of Basic Control Commands for AAI Teams—cont'd*

| Command | Command Description | Example Image of Command |
|---|---|---|
| "Come" | Dog is instructed to immediately move in front of or next to the handler. | |
| "Leave it" | Dog is instructed to ignore an interesting object such as food. | |
| "Controlled walk" | Dog is able to walk next to handler in a "heel" position (the dog is walking directly in step with the handler's heel) or on a leash (the leash is relaxed, indicating the dog is not pulling). | |

*Note:* While present in the health care facility, the handler must always hold onto the leash.

tolerate "clumsy petting" like that received during interactions with patients with limited dexterity. A dog must tolerate "rough embraces," such as those potentially offered when greeted by an excited young child. Additionally a dog must be able to react calmly to wheelchairs, walkers, canes, and medical equipment commonly encountered in a health care facility. Reactions to these scenarios can shed light on the dog's fitness to participate in AAI in your health care environment. Testing should include watching the dog's reaction to novel stimuli: how the dog reacts to loud noises and how the dog reacts to greeting and meeting strangers. Some tests may include the opening and closing of an umbrella, or rattling a metal bucket, to assess response to novel visual and auditory stimuli. How well a dog reacts to these scenarios can help to predict their reactions to the many novel stimuli they will inevitably encounter in a health care facility.

Equally important, the evaluation must also include the behavior of the therapy dog handler and the interaction between dog and handler. Handlers must be constantly attentive to their dogs, communicate clearly and appropriately (e.g., not harshly) with their dogs, maintain constant control over their dogs, and monitor their dogs' needs and well-being.

## 3.2 Human Requirements

All team handlers participating in AAI should fulfill the requirements of a volunteer working in your health care facility. AAI programs should work closely with the designated office that oversees volunteer activities in order to comply with rules and regulations applied to volunteers. At a minimum, volunteers should complete the following items (see Table 2) in order to participate in an AAI program.

TABLE 2 *Recommended Volunteer Requirements for AAI Teams*

| Requirement | Requirement Description |
|---|---|
| Human vaccinations | Individuals should be up to date on all vaccinations recommended by the health care facility (e.g., Varicella, Tdap, MMR, Hepatitis B, Meningococcal, Influenza). |
| Orientation | Individuals should complete orientation to the facility. This orientation should provide an overview of the facility and visitation areas. |
| Patient confidentiality | Individuals should complete training in HIPAA.* |
| Background check | Individuals should submit to and pass a background check. Those who fail a criminal background check should be excluded from participation. |
| Human health | Individuals cannot volunteer when ill with potentially communicable diseases. |

*Health Insurance Portability and Accountability Act of 1996.

## 3.3 Orientation and Training of AAI Teams

After AAI teams have met all program entry requirements, orientation to your health care facility and facility-specific training will increase the likelihood of successful visitation and retention of AAI teams. While both the human (through a designated volunteer services office at the health care facility) and the dog (through a therapy animal registration organization) have likely received instruction on interacting as an AAI team and volunteering in a health care facility, orientation is important in order to familiarize them to your particular facility and the areas approved for AAI.

An AAI program manual, such as the online downloadable template (docs.lib.purdue.edu/AAI) available with this manual, with all rules, regulations, policies, and procedures

**Figure 5** Two new AAI teams prepare for dog and handler shadowing. (Photo by Rebecca A. Vokes.)

should be provided to each AAI team upon admission to your program. This manual should be updated as program revisions are made, and all teams made aware of any changes in policy and procedures immediately.

Shadowing, or following an experienced AAI team visiting a patient at the facility, is recommended as an important component of orienting new AAI teams (see Figure 5). Shadowing without their own therapy dog provides new handlers with an opportunity to become familiar with the facility and observe how AAI is conducted at your particular facility. It can also be an opportunity to ask questions and address any confusion before the new handler is in the environment with his or her own dog. Shadowing shows the new handler how AAI program policies and procedures are implemented, providing a real-life demonstration of AAI to facilitate skill building, comfort, and safety in your health care facility.

The first visit by both the dog and handler to a facility should be accompanied by an experienced member of the AAI program. This not only provides support to ensure that the new team is comfortable and able to navigate safely on their first day, but also allows another chance to make sure that this team is appropriate for visitation in the facility. Careful observation for signs of stress in both the handler and in their dog should be conducted, and if present, immediately addressed.

# 4

# Establishing Requirements: AAI Implementation

Clear procedures must be established by your AAI program to maximize patient, staff, visitor, and AAI team safety and to enhance patient satisfaction. Since therapy dog organizations vary in the AAI procedures required of their members, health care facilities are strongly advised to consider the recommended procedures in this manual and included in the available online template (docs.lib.purdue.edu/AAI). These procedures are best communicated to your AAI teams through a hard copy and/or online manual (see Chapter 5, Section 5.4: Manuals for AAI Teams). AAI procedures must also be communicated to health care facility staff to inform them of the process and their roles in contributing to safe and efficient AAI team visits. All policies and procedures recommended in this manual are informed by evidence-based guidance regarding animals in health care settings, including the Society for Healthcare Epidemiology of America (Murthy et al. 2015). As more evidence becomes available, health care administrators are advised to continually revisit current epidemiological literature in order to update policies and procedures for AAI.

## 4.1 Health and Grooming

Policies should be established to ensure that each dog participating in AAI is healthy, well groomed, and bathed within 24 hours of visiting the health care facility. First, such policies minimize the entry of contaminates from the outside environment into the health care facility (thus protecting patients, staff, and visitors). Second, they provide the opportunity for the therapy dog handler to examine the dog for any wounds, sensitive spots, or areas of concern that might prevent them from visiting safely. And third, such policies set an important health and cleanliness standard. Concerns about health and grooming of a dog visiting in the facility should result in the immediate departure of the AAI team from the health care facility. AAI program staff should maintain open communication with health care facility employees, encouraging any staff member with a concern about dog grooming or health to contact AAI program staff immediately.

Table 3 can be used to inform your AAI teams and facility staff of the health and grooming requirements for therapy dog team presence in your facility on any given day. This list was developed to minimize risk of infection or incident, as well as provide guidance on safety, behavior, and appropriate grooming. Such guidelines are formed with input from infection control specialists, veterinarians, and therapy animal organizations in order to better ensure that AAI teams are healthy and prepared to visit, all while posing minimal risk to those in the acute health care facility.

TABLE 3 *Previsit Requirements for AAI Teams*

| Requirement | Requirement Description |
|---|---|
| Bathing | Dogs must be bathed and groomed within 24 hours of the visit. |
| Health | Dogs must be free of illness and/or infection. |
| Skin and coat | Dogs must be free of wounds/sores and have a healthy coat and skin. |
| Nails | Dogs must have nails trimmed as closely as possible. |
| Obedience | Dogs must be well behaved and firmly under the handler's control at all times. |
| Flea/tick collars | Dogs must not wear flea collars. |
| Flea/tick medication | Dogs must not be treated with flea medication (e.g., Frontline, Advantix) within 3 days of the visit. |
| Estrus (female dogs) | Female dogs must not visit while in estrus. |
| Raw diets | Dogs must not have been fed a raw diet within at least 90 days of visitation. |
| Pork products | Dogs must not have consumed "pork hide" or "pig ear" treats within at least 90 days of visitation. |
| Wellness check | AAI teams must provide documentation of a yearly wellness check signed by their veterinarian. |
| Vaccination | AAI teams must provide documentation of current immunizations signed by their veterinarian. |

## 4.2 Identification of Animals and Handlers and Security

For patients, staff, and visitors to identify AAI teams approved to enter the health care facility, teams must be easily identifiable. The volunteer AAI handler should wear an approved identification badge on the outermost layer of clothing, readily visible on the chest. A clothing uniform for the handler (this can simply be a designated shirt), and an identifying vest or bandana for the dog are ideal in order to maintain a clear and recognized presence while in a health care facility. The badge, shirt, and vest serve to verify and brand the use of AAI teams within your health care facility (see Figures 6 and 7). Proper identification should be provided for the AAI team, both person and dog, in accordance with your facility rules.

Staff, including security, should be made aware of the uniform designating an AAI team, and facilities must determine whether they would like to uniform AAI teams identically to other hospital volunteers. Identifying apparel (see Figures 6 and 7) that may be worn by AAI teams include the following:

**Dogs**
- Vest or bandana denoting therapy dog status
- Collar with visible rabies vaccination tag and/or therapy dog tag
- Leash denoting therapy dog status

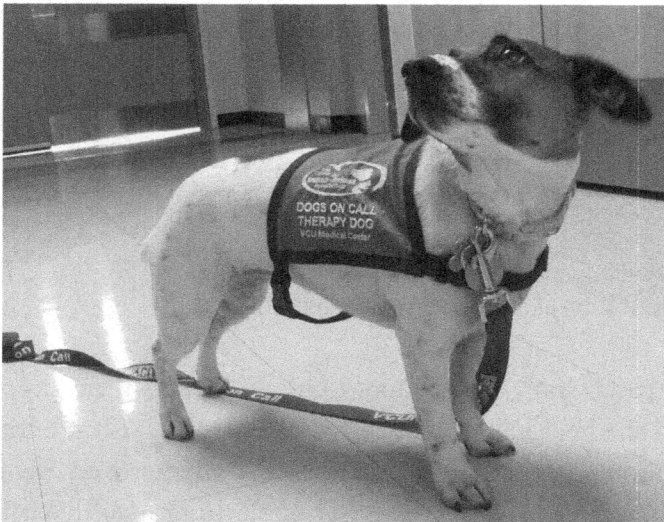

Figure 6 A therapy dog in uniform. (Photo by Rebecca A. Vokes.)

**Humans**
- Identification badge denoting volunteer status
- Uniform shirt (preferably with program name and indication of volunteer status)

Your facility may have areas where restrictions on access will require volunteers to have an access code or be escorted by personnel with access to the area. Your facility must determine the level of clearance for AAI teams, and outfit them with proper security devices that may allow them to access patient areas while volunteering. Any access-related concerns can be explained in the AAI manual for volunteers in order to prevent issues with security and safety in the hospital.

**Figure 7** A therapy dog handler and therapy dog in uniform. (Photo by Lucy Stefani.)

## 4.3 Arrival and Departure at the Facility

A safe parking area is important for AAI teams so that they may easily transport their animals to and from the health care facility. This area may include convenient access to an area where dogs may relieve themselves before entering the facility. Some facilities may offer complimentary parking, street parking, or another area where teams may park their vehicles.

It is important for your AAI program to maintain an active log of the visits made by AAI teams. Not only does this aid in program scheduling and evaluation, but it is also vital for the safety of teams and those individuals in your facility in the case of emergencies or adverse events. The log may be a paper sign-in sheet kept in a central location such as the Volunteer Office, accessible to all teams, or electronic via a computer system designated and accessible by the volunteers. The log provides a record of who is present in the facility at any given time, and enables safe management of the number of AAI teams at your health care facility. Finally, signing in and out is important in order to provide necessary tracking information in the unlikely occurrence of any adverse events or contact tracing needed for infectious disease. These policies should be communicated clearly to AAI teams (see Chapter 5, Section 5.4: Manuals for AAI Teams).

Electronic logs in Microsoft Excel or Access format can easily generate reports on visitation frequency and location. Consultation with health care facility's technology services department may provide additional solutions for tracking AAI team visitation.

## 4.4 Areas Approved for AAI

Your AAI program should develop clear policies regarding where AAI is permitted and consult with individual units in order to define areas of service and unit staff willing to serve as liaisons to the AAI program. These areas may include specific patient locations (such as the palliative care unit) as well as public areas such as lobbies, general hallways, outdoor areas, and waiting rooms.

Within these approved AAI areas, there may be certain rooms or zones where a therapy dog is not be permitted. For instance, although an AAI team may be allowed to visit patients and staff on a cardiac ICU floor, the kitchen area on that floor should be off-limits to the AAI team. Some AAI areas may include restrictions or limits, such as certain hours or days, or allow AAI only in response to requests from a physician in charge of a patient's care. AAI teams should always be prohibited in areas where sterility must be maintained (in operating rooms, preoperative suites, etc.), and in isolation rooms. Within all patient rooms, the AAI team should be prohibited from patient lavatories.

While it is important that your AAI program provide clear communication to AAI teams on where visitation is allowed and restricted, it is also important to inform unit staff of where AAI teams are prohibited on their unit. For example, if a nurse is on a lunch break eating a meal in the unit break room, and sees a visiting AAI team in the hallway, the nurse will know to exit the food preparation area in order to interact with the dog rather than inviting the AAI team into this area.

Particularly in large facilities, it is also advisable to provide unit maps to AAI teams identifying areas where they are allowed, restricted, or prohibited. These can be color-coded, such as using green highlighting to designate areas approved for visitation, red highlighting to designate areas restricted from visitation, and yellow highlighting to designate areas needing special permission for visitation, and laminated for ease of use.

## 4.5 Entering and Exiting Patient Areas

Unit staff should always be aware of the presence of a dog in order to maintain safe and orderly interactions with AAI teams. AAI policies and procedures should include instructions regarding appropriate protocol for entering patient areas. For example, when arriving to a unit, it is advisable that the therapy dog handler notify key staff on the unit. This can be as simple as approaching the nurse's station upon arrival to notify the nurse in charge or unit secretary of the AAI team's presence.

Unit staff may be readily able to identify patients who might be interested in a visit from the AAI team. Staff can also inform the AAI team of the location of linen and linen disposal in the event a towel or blanket is needed to provide a barrier between the therapy dog and patients requesting the dog be placed on their beds.

Unit staff may at times prohibit visitation with any patient based on the patient's medical condition or when a unit environment has an unusually high patient acuity level or limited staffing. Additionally, the AAI handler must be instructed to always obtain a verbal consent from the patient or from a responsible party in the patient's room before entering, as a patient's willingness to participate in AAI may have changed due to any number of factors including a change in mood, a change in medical condition, an additional family visit, and so on. In semiprivate rooms, permission must be obtained from all other patients in the room as well.

Just as it is important for unit staff to know when an AAI team is on their unit, they also need to be made aware of when the team is leaving. The AAI team can be instructed to simply alert staff at the nurses' station as they prepare to leave the unit. AAI teams also need to be informed of procedures for notifying staff of any pertinent information from the visit (for example, if a patient was not visited because they were sleeping, or a patient expressed fear of dogs) or of patient requests (for water, food, or any type of assistance).

## 4.6 Interactions With Patients

The key goal of any complementary therapy program in the health care facility is to improve the health and well-being of the patients.

While it is important to make AAI enjoyable and comforting for patients, it is vital that patient safety is always maintained. AAI programs must form and enforce policies and procedures that reduce the chance of infection or harm to a patient.

Any patient interacting with an AAI team should first have sanitized hands. This can be achieved by washing hands with warm water and antibacterial soap, or using health care facility approved hand sanitizer. AAI handlers must also sanitize their hands before interacting with a patient. AAI teams need to be informed of procedures for obtaining hand sanitizing products on each unit they visit. If hand sanitation products on a unit are immobile (such as wall dispensers) mobile products should be provided to AAI teams in order to allow them to sanitize the hands of those interacting with their dog. Ideally, multiuse, mobile, health care facility approved hand sanitizer should be provided to each AAI team and replenished as needed.

Unit staff may confer with the AAI team prior to any interactions with patients, especially on units where patients are likely to be injured or have physical areas of concern. Upon initial contact with a patient, the AAI handler should be instructed to visibly scan any exposed skin for scratches, cuts, or areas where any invasive devices are present on the patient. Contact with these areas must be avoided. AAI teams should be instructed to always be aware of patient comfort and the therapy dog's physical position.

AAI handlers may encourage patients to talk to their dogs and, if interested, pet their dogs, but also be open to having patients simply observe their dogs. At times it may be appropriate to let the dog lie on a patient's bed. When patients give verbal permission or express a desire for therapy dogs to lie on their beds, a towel or sheet must be used to cover the area where the dog will lie to provide a protective barrier between the dog and bedding. Unit staff should be aware of this policy and provide linens on request during AAI visits and directions for disposing of them after individual use.

The following behaviors illustrated in Table 4 are common in dog and human interactions, but should be discouraged in a health care setting to minimize risk of infection:

After any interaction with the AAI team, patients should once again sanitize their hands by washing with warm water and antibacterial soap, or using facility-approved sanitizer. AAI handlers should also sanitize their own hands after interacting with each patient.

## 4.7 Interactions With Families, Visitors, and Staff

There are many additional people present in the health care environment who may benefit from AAI. While interactions with AAI teams naturally occur with families and visitors of patients, the same procedures regarding hand hygiene must be observed during interactions with these individuals. Hands of all visitors and family members should be sanitized before and after interactions with the AAI team. The same interaction procedures appropriate with patients should be followed with families, visitors, and staff to minimize risk to these individuals, and to the patients with whom they come into contact.

## 4.8 Interactions With Staff

Employees of a health care facility often enjoy and benefit from AAI, and have been shown to experience reductions in stress as a result of even brief interactions with a therapy dog (see Figure 8). Some employees have scheduled their work shifts to coincide with when AAI is scheduled on their units.

On units where AAI teams visit frequently, the staff will also have the chance to see and interact with the dogs. These

**TABLE 4** *Behaviors to Avoid for AAI Teams*

| Behavior | Behavior Description | Example Image of Behavior |
|---|---|---|
| Licking | Licking behavior increases the chance of infection due to contact with the dog's mouth. Handlers should be particularly aware of sites of injury on a patient where a dog may sniff or lick. | |
| Pawing | A dog's pawing behavior increases risk of possible scratching. Paws are also a point on the dog's body where more contaminants may be found (due to their consistent contact with the ground), and patient contact with paws should be avoided. | |
| Jumping up on others | Jumping of dogs increases the likelihood of scratching, and also can lead to a fall that could result in injury to the patient. A dog's jumping may also be seen as disruptive to staff and visitors. | |

*Continued*

TABLE 4 *Behaviors to Avoid for AAI Team Manuals—cont'd*

| Behavior | Behavior Description | Example Image of Behavior |
|---|---|---|
| Touching the nose and mouth of dog | It is important to minimize contact with the mouth and paws of the dog, as these are potential sites of infection transmission from dog to person. Individuals should be encouraged to pet the dog on the back and body. | |
| Playing in a rough manner | Playing in a rough manner greatly increases the likelihood that a scratch, fall, or even a "mouthing" or "play nip" could occur from the dog. This manner of interaction is not appropriate for an acute health care setting. | |

Photos by Rebecca A. Vokes.

staff members will often assist in identifying patients in their care who they think will enjoy a visit. It should be noted that staff interacting with AAI teams should follow the same procedures as any patient or visitor, particularly with hand sanitizing. As in the general population, many employees will have pets at home and may benefit from reminders of proper procedures for interacting with therapy dogs in the health care facility. Organizing an educational meeting or workshop for staff where AAI will be permitted is ideal, and will give AAI program staff the opportunity to explain AAI policies and procedures, as well as an opportunity to answer any questions from unit staff. Consider

**Figure 8** A nurse pauses during her shift to visit with an AAI team. One study reported that interactions with therapy dogs as brief as 5 minutes may produce a similar physiological stress reduction to a 20-minute break for health care professionals. (Photo by Jordan Vance.)

consulting with managers on units where AAI teams will occur in order to best serve their staff. Some units may house patient populations not suitable for AAI (surgical units, bone marrow transplant units, etc.), therefore it is recommended that health care facilities identify ways to provide opportunities for all interested members of staff to interact with therapy dogs. This may involve arranging for AAI to occur in a break room, or providing special events for staff and the public to attend and interact with therapy dogs.

Equally important is for unit managers to identify staff with allergies to dog dander, fear of dogs, or discomfort with dogs' presence so that measures can be taken to meet staff needs. Such measures may include limiting AAI to a designated location on the unit, scheduling a staff member's shift around the AAI schedule, and ensuring the AAI schedule for the unit is prominently displayed.

## 4.9 Infectious Disease Prevention Summary

Table 5 provides a summary of current infectious disease prevention guidelines for therapy dog owners and their handlers from the Society for Healthcare Epidemiology of America (SHEA, personal communication, August 22, 2018) and are incorporated into this manual. A short description of each guideline is provided.

**TABLE 5** *Current Infectious Disease Prevention Guidelines for AAI in Health Care Settings*

| Category | Category Description |
|---|---|
| Hand Hygiene | Hand hygiene should be performed by the patient or health care personnel before and after interacting with the dog. Handlers should follow the hospital hand hygiene policy. |
| Handler Health | Dog handlers should not participate in AAI while ill with respiratory symptoms (cough, upper respiratory symptoms), fever, diarrhea or vomiting, conjunctivitis, rash, or non-intact skin on areas that cannot be covered. |
| Dog Health | All dogs participating in AAI should undergo regular veterinary wellness checks and stool evaluations and remain current on vaccinations for rabies, *Bordetella bronchiseptica*, and leptospirosis. Additionally, dogs suffering from any illness, skin and coat conditions, or any other wound should not participate in AAI until cleared by a veterinarian. |
| Dog Dietary Restrictions | Dogs should not be fed raw foods, chews, or treats of animal origin. If such foods have been fed, dogs should not visit for at least 90 days. |
| Restricted Areas | Dogs should be restricted from isolation rooms, food handling areas, ICUs, and other areas based upon hospital policy. |
| Invasive Devices | Dogs should not come in contact with invasive devices, wounds, surgical incisions or medical equipment. |
| Interactions | Patients and health care personnel should not have contact with the dog's paws, nose, or mouth. Barriers should be used when dogs interact on patient beds. |
| Contact Tracing | Records should be kept documenting the dates, areas, and room numbers where dogs have interacted with patients to allow contact tracing for any concerns related to exposure to communicable diseases. |
| Environmental Cleaning | Routine cleaning and disinfection of surfaces should be performed after visits. |
| Health Records | Health records for both dogs and humans participating in AAI should be kept in a secure location. |

# 5

# Maintaining Compliance: Renewals, Record Keeping, and Team Retention

Health care administrators have a responsibility to ensure the safety, reliability, and accountability of AAI programs. This means that records must be kept of all AAI teams, documenting current handler information, therapy dog registration, health records of both human and dog, renewals, and any supplementary training or records of reinstatement. Maintaining appropriate documentation of AAI team compliance is needed for Joint Commission on the Accreditation of Healthcare Organizations (JCAHO) and other credentialing reviews as well as for examining any adverse events. During a recent JCAHO review at the authors' facility, therapy dog team records were requested as part of the review and lauded by the review team for the documentation included (and recommended in this chapter).

If an AAI team's registration with a therapy dog organization is expiring, or the AAI team is noncompliant with your AAI program/health care facility standards, options for renewal, reinstatement, or retirement should be presented to the handler.

Over time, health and compliance of an AAI team can change. For instance, while a dog may be very well behaved initially on a geriatric unit where wheelchairs are present, if the dog is at home and his tail is accidently rolled over by a wheelchair, he could develop a fear. This dog may react differently to wheelchairs from then on, and a subsequent evaluation could identify the behavior change. A dog's health may change over time, and it is important to identify any new or progressing health concerns that may influence the dog's behavior, negatively impact their well-being, or have an impact on the safety of others in the health care facility (such as in the event of infection).

## 5.1 Records and Registration

Proof of compliance should be kept for each AAI team active in your facility, and at no time should an AAI team's presence be permitted in your facility without proof of compliance with all standards for AAI teams outlined in your policies and procedures. A copy of records for each individual volunteering as an AAI team should be kept by your AAI program, and also by your office overseeing volunteers.

The following documentation should be obtained for each AAI team:

- registration with approved therapy animal group (see Figure 9);
- records of registration renewals and reevaluations,

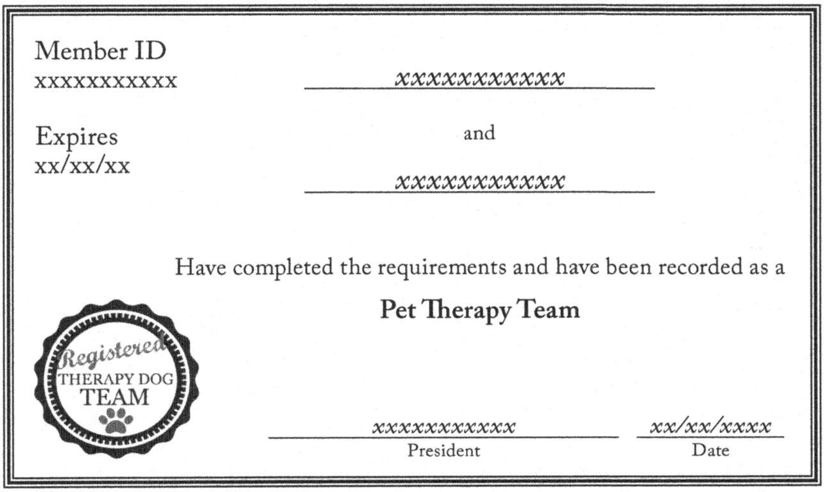

Member ID
xxxxxxxxxxx

_____ *xxxxxxxxxxx* _____

Expires
xx/xx/xx

and

_____ *xxxxxxxxxxx* _____

Have completed the requirements and have been recorded as a

**Pet Therapy Team**

_____ *xxxxxxxxxxx* _____ *xx/xx/xxxx*
President           Date

**Figure 9** Example of a therapy dog registration card noting the handler, the dog, and the expiration date of their registration.

- records of subsequent shadowing and observations with the AAI program,
- records of any adverse events and subsequent retraining, and
- annual veterinary health verification including negative fecal test results and vaccination dates (see Figure 10).

An electronic database may be developed by your AAI program in order to organize and provide easy access to important team information and monitor compliance. Name, contact, registration status, dog breed and name, and important dates may be kept in a data program such as Microsoft Excel (see Figures 11 and 12).

Informing AAI teams of these requirements in the AAI manual and providing appropriate forms for collection of the information facilitate compliance. The downloadable online manual template (docs.lib.purdue.edu/AAI) includes this information.

## Program Health Verification Form

This registered therapy dog is participating in animal-assisted activity and/or animal-assisted therapy at ABC Health Care Facility.

Dog owner's name: _____ Phone: _____

Address: _____

Dog's name: _____

Date of annual wellness exam: _____

Date of current **negative** fecal exam: _____

Date of current rabies vaccination: _____

☐ 1 year      ☐ 3 year

Or rabies titer within last 2 years: _____ Titer level: _____

Veterinarian name: _____

Veterinarian address: _____

Veterinarian phone: _____

I have examined the dog indicated on this form within the last 12 months and believe the dog to be healthy and free of internal and external parasites on the date listed above.

_____      _____

Required veterinarian signature           Date

**Figure 10** Example health verification form providing proof of health and vaccinations should be kept in the offices of the AAI program.

| Last Name | First Name | Dog Name | Date Joined AAI Program | Dog Breed | Phone | Email |
|-----------|-----------|----------|------------------------|-----------|-------|-------|
| Smith | John | Cameo | 2/15/2016 | Husky | xxx-xxxx | xxxxxx@xxxxxxxx.com |
| Doe | Jane | Lemonade | 12/22/2014 | Golden Retriever | xxx-xxxx | xxxxxx@xxxxxxxx.com |
| Smith | Olivia | Oliver | 5/24/2015 | Spaniel Mix | xxx-xxxx | xxxxxx@xxxxxxxx.com |

**Figure 11** Example of a simple database containing membership and contact information of AAI teams.

| | | Therapy Dog Registration | | Annual Health Verification | | | |
|-----------|-----------|--------------------------|-----------------|---------------------|------------------------|------------------|------------------------|
| Last Name | First Name | Dog Name | Organization | Expiration Date | Rabies (1 or 3 yr?) | Negative Fecal Test | Wellness Visit | Date of Annual Shadowing |
| Smith | John | Cameo | Approved Therapy Dog Organization | 2/28/2016 | 04/2016 (3 yr) | 3/16/2015 | 3/16/2015 | 8/14/2017 |
| Doe | Jane | Lemonade | Approved Therapy Dog Organization | 8/6/2017 | 01/2016 (3 yr) | 8/21/2015 | 8/21/2015 | 8/14/2017 |
| Smith | Olivia | Oliver | Approved Therapy Dog Organization | 11/23/2017 | 02/2017 (1 yr) | 4/15/2016 | 4/15/2016 | 8/14/2017 |

**Figure 12** Example of an AAI team compliance database with information on the fulfillment of requirements for therapy dog teams.

## 5.2 Renewal, Reinstatement, and Retirement

After initially fulfilling the requirements to participate in AAI as a therapy dog team, renewals should be required for both dog and handler. As vaccinations and health testing expire, records for both humans (through the office overseeing human volunteers at your health care facility) and their dogs (through delivery of veterinary records to your AAI program) should be monitored on a regular basis for compliance with up-to-date documentation. Any AAI team not in compliance with all records should not be permitted to visit the health care facility until they provide this documentation to achieve compliance.

Renewal requirements for maintaining registration in external therapy animal organizations vary. While some organizations may require an evaluation of training and temperament to renew a registration, others only require a passive form of renewal (such as payment of annual dues). Health care administrators are strongly advised to select an organization requiring a reevaluation of therapy dog health, behavior, and temperament at least every other year.

It is also advisable that AAI programs institute their own process for evaluating AAI teams on a continuing basis to verify that they are still appropriate for visiting in the facility and complying with your policies and procedures. This may take the form of a shadowing requirement for all AAI teams to be conducted on a yearly basis. This procedure allows your AAI program to verify appropriateness for program participation as well as identify any changes in behavior and training that may need to be addressed. These shadowings may be conducted by AAI staff or by your more experienced AAI volunteers in a leadership role.

Your policies should clearly state that AAI teams that fail to renew their qualifications will be prohibited from entering your facility until reinstatement occurs. Reinstatement procedures may vary depending on the reason the team is no longer in compliance. For example, if a team fails to provide proof of vaccination by submitting a health verification form within one year of their last veterinary visit, the team may be asked not to visit until this record has been submitted. Failure to provide proof of reevaluation or renewal of therapy dog registration may follow the same reinstatement process.

Occasionally, a dog working as an AAI team may develop a behavioral issue. Factors such as maturing/aging, changes in diet, exercise, routine, or health, and adverse events or experiences can result in a change in a dog's behavior. AAI teams should be encouraged to look out for behavioral changes, and self-report them when necessary. Examples of common behavioral issues are:

- vocalizing excessively (barking, yelping, whining, or howling),
- pulling on leash,
- reacting adversely to other dogs,
- reacting adversely to equipment or environmental stimuli, and
- jumping (on people, or on objects).

Program staff may learn of a behavioral issue from a staff member, visitor, or in some cases, a patient. Program staff may also learn of a behavioral issue occurring at an offsite location. The following procedures can be helpful when responding to a potential behavioral issue.

First, contact the volunteer immediately, inform him or her of the issue raised, and temporarily suspend the team from entering the facility while the issue is being addressed. Second, the issue should be documented in the AAI team's record, and the handler advised to seek outside training from a credentialed dog trainer or animal behaviorist. Third, for reinstatement, a letter from the trainer or animal behaviorist should be required, documenting training completion and attesting that the dog is appropriate to return to normal visitation in the facility. It is also advisable for the AAI team to be subsequently shadowed in the health care facility to make sure all dog behavior is appropriate. Please note, any behavioral issue in which the dog shows signs of aggression or territoriality should result in retirement of the dog from the AAI program, as this type of behavior could lead to an adverse event including a dog bite.

Over time, it is natural for teams to retire. Retirement is typically initiated by the handler due to changes such as aging of the dog, time constraints on the volunteer, or moving away from their current city. However, some handlers may not recognize signs indicating the dog is no longer appropriate for visiting. Signs that a dog may be ready to retire from therapy work include

- slowing down (the dog is unable to keep up with owner at a normal pace, and seems lethargic on visits),
- exhibiting health issues (common health problems associated with aging including arthritis/joint problems, mobility difficulties, decreasing vision, and hearing loss), and
- declining attention and responsiveness.

It is important to be mindful of aging, and the annual AAI team shadowing provides an opportunity to assess fitness for continued therapy dog work.

Records for retiring AAI teams may be kept for a 12-month period in case any questions arise. Some type of recognition or celebration for retiring dogs can also be arranged to recognize the contributions the dogs and handlers have made to the AAI program and health care facility.

## 5.3 AAI Team Retention and Celebration

AAI programs and the health care facilities in which they operate invest considerable time and resources bringing volunteers on board to visit with patients, families, and staff. Just like in the health care workforce, volunteer dissatisfaction can lead to less effective care and turnover. Since payment is not an incentive for work as an AAI team, keeping volunteers in any program can be challenging. Regular communication with teams is key to building and maintaining strong relationships with the facility and staff. Scheduling enjoyable events for the AAI teams, which may include their families, provides a way for them to come together and socialize, either with or without their dogs. Whether a picnic is planned for an outdoor park (see Figure 13) with dogs included, a service event in the community bringing the AAI teams together to represent the organization (see Figure 14), or a meeting in a facility conference room without dogs, such events provide an opportunity to show appreciation for teams, obtain feedback about the program, and provide program updates.

Providing opportunities for continuing AAI education provides additional support that benefits the health care facility and adds value to volunteering. Instruction on recognizing the signs of stress in dogs and reading dog body language is important when relying on AAI teams to operate safely and cohesively. For example, a training module on dog body language is available through Pet Partners (see Additional Resources). Such training is also of interest and valued by AAI handlers. Increasing AAI team awareness of published research showing benefits of AAI promotes pride in their work and evidence of the positive impact they have on those they visit. Making training and educational resources available to teams contributes to their professional

**Figure 13** A group of AAI teams gathers for an outdoor picnic. (Photo by Randolph T. Barker.)

**Figure 14** AAI teams congregate in a common area to meet and greet during a public service event. (Photo by Tyler Zufall.)

development, communicates value in what they contribute, and enhances safety in the health care facility.

AAI teams are subject to compassion fatigue, just like others who work in health care facilities. Visiting children and adults with acute, chronic, and/or terminal illnesses can take an emotional toll on volunteers. Unlike health care employees, volunteers do not have access to staff debriefings, employee assistance programs, and other avenues of support. Developing strategies to provide support will reduce potential burnout and increase retention. One option is to collaborate with an existing department offering mental health services (social work, patient counseling, psychiatry, etc.) in the health care facility to provide a support group periodically. Developing relationships with community mental health professionals who may be willing to voluntarily provide a monthly support group is another option. If funding is available, a mental health professional in the community may be willing to provide a support group. Designated time at an AAI meeting can also be used to educate volunteers about compassion fatigue and self-care strategies and generate discussion about the impact of visiting patients.

An additional strategy to retain AAI teams is to set up a recognition system for visitation. Levels based on volunteer hours or years in the program can be used to provide modest gifts or special badges (e.g., Senior AAI team). Verbally expressing appreciation to AAI teams publicly and privately at every opportunity goes a long way in supporting retention. Such recognition acknowledges the effort that goes into training and qualifying dogs to join the AAI program, the work involved in readying a dog for every visit, the cost of veterinary care, and the many benefits their visits bring to patients, families, visitors, and staff.

## 5.4 Manuals for AAI Teams

One of the most important functions of the AAI program staff is to clearly communicate AAI policies and procedures to those who will provide AAI in your health care facility. Through orientation, training, and shadowing, the AAI staff communicates these policies and procedures to AAI teams. However, during most encounters AAI teams have with patients and visitors in the health care facility, they may be unaccompanied by a member of AAI staff. Therefore, it is very important for an AAI program to translate all policies and procedures into a comprehensive manual that each volunteer can consult. The downloadable online manual (docs.lib.purdue.edu/AAI) for AAI volunteers that accompanies this print manual includes the print recommendations and can be tailored to your facility. It should be a clear expectation of your program that volunteers read and understand AAI policies as communicated in the manual.

Table 6 outlines suggested manual sections and content for AAI programs to provide to teams. Please note that this manual should also include informational sections to familiarize volunteers with your AAI programming, facility and areas they will visit, and any other supplementary materials that could enhance their AAI service. This manual should also be updated annually to reflect the most current program policies and procedures.

**TABLE 6** *Section Recommendations for AAI Team Manuals*

| Section | Section Description |
|---|---|
| Introduction and Welcome | The introduction in your volunteer manual gives staff an opportunity to welcome new AAI teams, establish areas of service, outline opportunities, and further explain expectations of participation. Depending on the facility and time commitments, educational opportunities and other modes of volunteer participation may be highlighted in this section. |
| Contact Information | This section should include contact information for all program staff, as well as any other staff members at the health care facility who may be involved with the AAI program. Additional links may include a website, social media accounts, and other websites accessed by AAI teams on a regular basis. The section should also include a physical location of the program, phone number, and mailing address. |
| Definitions of Working Animals | All volunteers should be able to clearly define and explain the following terms: (a) service animal, (b) therapy animal, and (c) emotional support animal. These definitions familiarize volunteers with the field of human–animal interaction, and help to provide a basic understanding of the laws regarding the presence of animals in different service capacities. Each volunteer should fully understand the differences between therapy animals, service animals, and emotional support animals in order to act according to federal and state law, and in order to avoid misconceptions about their work as an AAI team (see Chapter 1, section 1.4, Key Definitions). |
| Requirements for Registration | This section clearly delineates the requirements that must be met to become a member of the AAI program, as well as the requirements that must be met to continue to remain an active member of the group. It may also provide copies of necessary documentation for teams to update on a scheduled basis in order to remain in compliance. |

*Continued*

TABLE 6 *Section Recommendations for AAI Team Manuals—cont'd*

| Section | Section Description |
| --- | --- |
| Visitation Procedures | This section will likely make up the majority of the manual text, and should include a comprehensive guide to policy and procedure for all therapy dog teams. Policy and procedure should at minimum include (a) previsitation requirements, (b) identification and apparel requirements, (c) signing in and/or out of the facility, (d) interactions with patients, and (e) interactions with staff, visitors, and family. This section provides the guidelines for proper AAI handling in an acute health care facility. Visitation rules should be developed with these goals in mind: (a) minimizing the risk of infection; (b) minimizing the risk of injury to patient, staff, visitor, or AAI team; (c) minimizing the stress of the animal while interacting at the facility; and (d) minimizing disruption of staff duties, patient treatment, and family/ guest visitation. Please see Chapter 4, "Establishing Requirements: AAI Implementation," for more information on suggested rules for AAI visitation. |
| Adverse Events | Adverse events are uncommon as a result of AAI, but possible in an acute care environment. It is important for AAI program staff to reinforce that in any given situation the role of an AAI team is to maintain control of their dog safely. Once this has been achieved, the team may ask for help in a way that is appropriate for your facility (e.g., pushing a call button or finding the nearest staff member for assistance). The most common adverse event is an accidental elimination. Conferring with service response staff and infection control, AAI program staff should identify the best method of responding to this event. After any adverse event concerning an AAI team, proper administration at the health care facility should be notified, and records should be kept of the event, the response, and preventative measures taken to lessen the likelihood of future adverse events. |
| Additional Notes | This section may contain additional information for AAI teams regarding media guidelines, HIPAA compliance, insurance and liability, retirement of AAI teams, and/or contact and communication methods. |

TABLE 6 *Section Recommendations for AAI Team Manuals—cont'd*

| Section | Section Description |
|---|---|
| References and Resources | This section acknowledges reference material for the manual text, and also lists outside resources for AAI teams. For example an animal stress resource should be provided to protect the well-being of the animal and to reduce the chance of a negative incident (which is more likely if an animal is stressed or fearful). AAI handlers should be educated on the signs of stress in their dogs, and AAI program staff should have a clear understanding of the signs of stress in dogs and how to address any issues that may arise as AAI teams visit in the environment. |
| Appendix Materials | This section should include any attachments that may be useful for AAI teams. Examples of possible attachments include maps of the health care facility coded to indicate areas approved for AAI visitation. |

# 6

# Program Evaluation

Program evaluation is often overlooked. However, program evaluation results can be critical in your management decisions about whether to fund or end a program. Evaluations can justify a program by showing the number of patients, families, and staff reached, the positive impact of the program on patients and staff, the cost-effectiveness and safety of the program, and external recognition of program value. Evaluations can also identify areas that may need improvement, leading to beneficial changes for the program.

The evaluation of an AAI program goes hand-in-hand with program development, implementation, and maintenance. In establishing a new program, goals should be identified, resources assessed, and processes and procedures pilot tested, evaluated, and revised as needed to improve the program for a particular facility. Once the AAI program is developed and implemented, evaluation activities should continue in order to provide important feedback regarding the value and effectiveness of the AAI program. Such information is critical for health care administrators in making decisions about continuing or revising the program and in making funding decisions.

Program evaluation is similar to empirical research and often uses some of the same methods; however, their purposes differ. Basic research aims to generate new knowledge or add to existing knowledge, typically by studying relationships among variables and/or determining cause-and-effect relationships. For example, research may explore the causes of cardiovascular disease or the relationship between obesity and diabetes. Applied research seeks to solve practical problems, such as improving access to health care or treating a specific disease. Evaluation aims to determine the worth or merit of a program. Evaluations describe programs and systematically collect information on which to base judgements regarding program effectiveness and the feasibility of programs. Ideally, evaluation takes place over the life of the program, from initially assessing the need for and feasibility of the program, to pilot and field testing procedures, to measuring program outcomes.

Evaluators may be internal to the program (a member of the AAI program staff) or external (a member of the health care facility staff or another external professional). External evaluators will need to work closely with program staff to understand the AAI program mission/aims, goals, procedures, and intended outcomes. Since most AAI programs are relatively small with limited resources, this chapter assumes evaluators will be internal and is written for evaluators familiar with the AAI program.

There are a number of program evaluation models. One very useful and popular model that will be summarized here is the Context, Input, Process, Product (CIPP) evaluation model originally developed by Daniel Stufflebeam (2007) and colleagues for evaluating educational programs in the 1960s. The model has subsequently been updated and applied to a wide variety of settings. The model was designed to accompany the different stages of program development, from identifying the need for the program to retrospectively determining the effectiveness of the program after implementation. While comprehensive, the model is flexible in that the different components of the CIPP model can be implemented based on the developmental stage of the program and feasibility. In this manual, The CIPP model will be summarized and applied to evaluating AAI programs in health care settings with examples for your facility. There are numerous articles available on the CIPP model for those interested in more detailed information. The reference list contains several citations.

For AAI programs in the initial planning stage, a *context evaluation* is useful in defining the environment in which the AAI program will be implemented and identifying the service opportunity or need the program will address. For example, an AAI program at the initial stage of development for a psychiatric service facility would benefit from conducting a context evaluation that would include a detailed description of the psychiatric service including the location, space, and layout of the service, number of beds, number and type of staff, type of patient served, and patient volume. The context evaluation would involve the psychiatry service leadership and staff in identifying the patient and/or or staff needs that AAI will address, such as patient anxiety, fear, boredom, or isolation and/or staff stress. Context evaluation may also include a survey of patients to assess their interest in such a program and a survey of management and staff to identify interest and concerns about implementing an AAI program. The latter survey would provide an indication of staff education that may be needed as well as potential issues the program will need to address. It is important that the results of the context evaluation be shared with all staff who will be involved in the program.

*Input evaluation* during AAI program development focuses on collecting needed information to determine if sufficient resources are available to establish the program and to define the strategies that will be used to implement the AAI program. The input evaluation may identify existing therapy dog organizations in the community that might be interested in collaborating with your health care facility to provide dog teams for the program. The input evaluation may also identify a staff person or persons who will help coordinate the schedule for visiting therapy dog teams on a particular service at times that are convenient for staff and complement the existing treatment schedule, identify patients appropriate to participate on a given program day, and availability to accompany the dog team while on the psychiatric service.

The *process evaluation* component focuses on assessing program activities. The evaluator observes the implementation of the program, keeping track of implementation progress, assessing whether policies and procedures are followed, noting what procedures work well and where problems are encountered. The evaluator may pilot test AAI procedures and follow one or two experienced therapy dog teams from the time they enter the facility to the time they leave to observe everything from clear identification of the therapy dog and handler being visible, to signing in and out appropriately, to asking permission to enter elevators and patient rooms, using hand sanitizer, and length of time visiting patients. The evaluator will observe patient, family, visitor, and staff interactions and responses and may informally ask them about their experience with the AAI and note positive and negative comments. The results of the process evaluation are shared with all involved parties and are used to decide whether to keep moving forward with the program, revise the program, or end the program.

The *product evaluation* assesses the impact of the program. The evaluator determines whether program goals are being met, including whether the intended recipients were reached and identifying intended and unintended outcomes, both positive and negative. The AAI program evaluator may assign someone to shadow a therapy dog team with a counter to identify how many patients participated in the program as well as how many family members, visitors, and staff interacted with therapy dog team. The evaluator may conduct surveys, interviews, or other assessments to determine if the AAI program achieved the program goals and whether AAI was associated with reduced anxiety in patients, reduced stress in staff, increased patient smiles and laughter, increased patient time spent interacting with other patients and staff, and so on. The evaluator will also want to determine if patients and/or staff other than those intended for the AAI program interacted with the therapy dog team. Therapy dogs are very popular and it is common for staff and visitors who see the team in common areas of the facility to request visits for their patients. Keeping track of such requests will be very helpful in determining if and where the AAI program may be expanded in the future.

It is also important to identify unintended outcomes of the program, both positive and negative. For example, did the AAI program interfere with other treatment taking place with the patients (occupational therapy, recreational therapy, etc.) or did the program result in patients requesting less medication? Resources required to operate the program are also important to assess to determine if the program is cost-effective. Results of the product evaluation provide valuable information about the extent to which AAI program goals are reached, aspects of the program that may be improved, and the adequacy of resource allocation. Such information is important in determining program value and effectiveness.

Program evaluation is a helpful tool not just to develop and implement a new AAI program, but also to maintain the program and provide continuing evidence of program impact and value. Periodic surveys, interviews, and/or observations can reveal if the program is being implemented as intended and also identify potential problems. These assessments should also include the therapy dog teams for their unique perspective on program operations. From member feedback, one facility found that having a meeting of all new therapy dog teams within the first few months of their joining the program provided an excellent opportunity to review procedures and answer questions. Member feedback also alerted the program staff that compassion fatigue may occur in teams visiting areas of a hospital experiencing patient mortality. Your putting activities in place to support therapy dog teams may help prevent compassion fatigue, potential burnout, and losing teams.

Results of ongoing evaluation can provide valuable information about the continuing demand for AAI and positive outcomes achieved. Such information provides evidence to justify requests for increased resources from your administration for program maintenance and expansion.

# 7

# Beyond Visitation: Animal-Assisted Therapy (AAT) and Facility Dogs

You will remember from previous chapters that animal-assisted activities (AAA) include therapy dog visitation and are referred to as AAT by many in the media and scholarly journals. However, there is a distinct difference between the two. AAA may mean any range of activities, and are often unstructured and serve to provide enjoyment, entertainment, and distraction from medical conditions and the medical environment. Although associated with many positive outcomes, including reductions in stress, anxiety, loneliness, depression, and pain in some patients, AAA is not delivered as part of a patient's care plan to reach treatment goals (see Figure 15). Below are examples of actual facility patient case experiences.

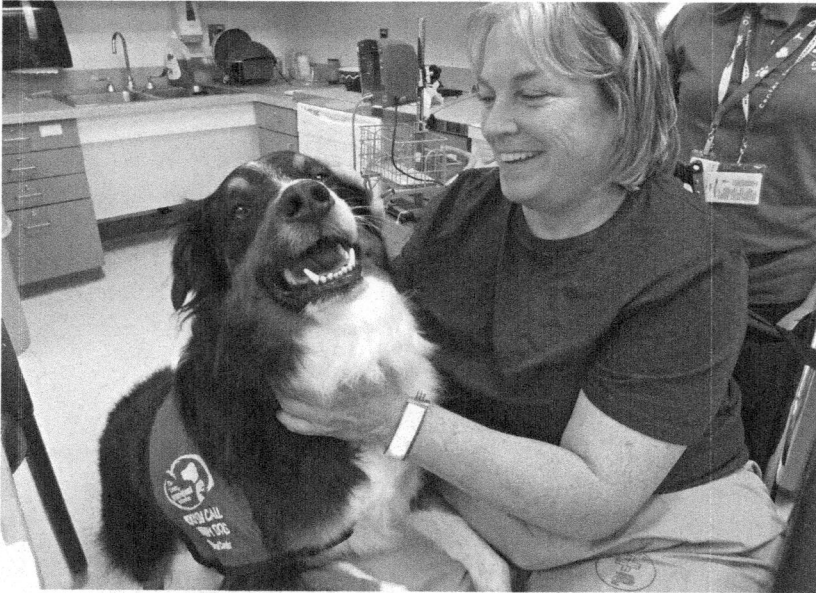

**Figure 15** A physical rehabilitation patient pets a therapy dog after completing a task during treatment. (Photo by Rebecca A. Vokes.)

## 7.1 Animal-Assisted Therapy (AAT)

A relatively new complementary therapy, AAT is structured to produce a desired outcome for a particular patient through interaction with the therapy dog. AAT is typically delivered by a health care professional and incorporated into a patient's care plan. AAT has the potential to contribute to many positive patient outcomes; however, more research is needed to identify what outcomes can be impacted in what settings and for which patients. AAT should have a documented treatment goal and be included with traditional interventions in the patient's medical record, along with the patient's response to the intervention and progress toward goal achievement. As an administrator you should consult with health care information technology staff and clinicians in order to determine how best to record AAT in the patient's electronic health record (EHR).

## 7.2 AAT Case Examples

*Case 1*

B. V. is a 29-year-old male with multiple fractures to both hands as the result of a fall while skiing. He underwent an operation to mend metacarpals and proximal phalanges in both hands, and is now undergoing regular physical therapy at the orthopedic rehabilitation unit. He is having trouble regaining the use of his dominant hand in particular, and often becomes visibly frustrated, sometimes even refusing to continue with a session. After discussing the case with the patient's care team, the physical therapist arranges for AAT at an upcoming session and incorporates the dog into exercises that encourage the use of patient's dominant hand. The patient shows increased motivation to use his dominant hand to toss a tennis ball across the room to the dog. The dog's retrieval of the ball, returning it to the patient and waiting for it to be thrown again, encourages the patient to repeat the exercise multiple times. After the AAT session, B. V. is asked for feedback on the exercise with the dog and expresses the desire to work with the dog again. The physical therapist schedules further AAT sessions. The goal is to increase the patient's participation in physical rehabilitation exercises, and to improve hand function by using the hand to pet the dog, brush the dog, and throw toys for the dog. The sessions are recorded in the provider notes section of B. V.'s EHR.

*Case 2*

S. H. is a 56-year-old female diagnosed with major depression and hospitalized after a suicide attempt. A dog lover, the patient is isolating herself in her room and interacting little with staff or other patients. Her psychiatrist requests AAT to encourage the patient to leave her room and interact more with other patients and staff. A licensed professional counselor in the facility's AAI program meets with the treatment team to discuss the AAT plan. She subsequently brings her therapy dog to the unit and encourages the patient to walk the dog in the hallway with her. As the patient walks the dog, holding one end of a double leash also held by the counselor, other patients and staff approach her to pet the dog and talk with the patient about the dog. The interaction is noted by the psychiatrist in her client notes.

## 7.3 Facility Dogs

Some health care facilities are interested in having a more constant presence of a dog on a particular service for longer periods of time than the hour or two typical for AAT or AAI. The intensive health care environment with high stimuli, unpredictability, multiple staff and patients, and unusual sounds and smells creates an unnatural and stressful environment for dogs. Advanced training is needed for dogs to work comfortably in such a setting for long periods of time. Some service dog organizations (e.g., Canine Companions for Independence) train facility dogs for this purpose. Facility dogs are expertly trained to work with a handler/facilitator in a setting specific to the handler's qualifications. Facility dogs are highly trained to reliably respond to numerous commands to facilitate a professional working with populations with special needs (see Figure 16).

Facility dogs may provide a calming and/or motivating presence for patients. While the facility dog may be onsite with its handler during the time period the handler is at work in the health care facility, the facility dog should accompany the handler home from

**Figure 16** This facility dog serves at an inpatient psychiatric unit for children. A facility dog can provide valuable animal-assisted interventions for an inpatient or residential population. (Photo by Lindy Rodman, VCU University Relations.)

the health care facility to live. Facility dogs should also meet the required qualifications set forth by the AAI program and provide records of facility dog training, any certifications, registrations, and veterinary information for the AAI program's records. As with therapy dogs, the welfare of the dog should be carefully monitored. Ample quiet times away from patients and other staff and exercise breaks must be carefully scheduled into every day the facility dog is present. Watching for signs of fatigue and stress, while primarily the responsibility of the dog's handler, should be done by all staff on site.

# Summary, Opportunity, and the Future

As administrators, you realize the importance of identifying key points to action as you move forward with the ideas presented in this manual. What may seem like a time-consuming task is easily addressed by downloading the online template for volunteer teams (docs.lib.purdue.edu/AAI) as you begin your process establishing an animal-assisted intervention (AAI) program within your health care facility.

You have now read about the benefits of AAI, examples of program structure, establishing requirements for your AAI program entry, the implementation of AAI, an approach for maintaining compliance through renewals, record keeping ideas, guidelines of team retention, and also the importance of program evaluation. The 10-year, real-world, time-tested health care facility program experience presented in this manual actually creates an opportunity for you and your team to add an evidence-based, low-cost, complementary therapy and also an organizational well-being addition to your human relations efforts (Barker, Knisely, Barker, Cobb, & Schubert, 2012).

The future in health care administration and the medical field provides many challenges and possibilities for creative problem solving. Your future vision including the use of AAI could be an answer to some of those unknowns. The evidence presented by human–animal interaction research allows you to be confident of the potential of this option in moving forward. We wish you much success in your decision to apply AAI in your organization.

# References

Abate, S. V., Zucconi, M., & Boxer, B. A. (2011). Impact of canine-assisted ambulation on hospitalized chronic heart failure patients' ambulation outcomes and satisfaction: A pilot study. *Journal of Cardiovascular Nursing, 26*(3), 224–230. https://doi.org/10.1097/JCN.0b013e3182010bd6

Allen, K., Shykoff, B. E., & Izzo, J. L., Jr. (2001). Pet ownership, but not ace inhibitor therapy, blunts home blood pressure responses to mental stress. *Hypertension, 38*(4), 815–820. Retrieved from https://www.ncbi.nlm.nih.gov/pubmed/11641292

American Veterinary Medical Association. (2018). Policies. Retrieved March 12, 2018, from https://www.avma.org/KB/policies

Bardill, N., & Hutchinson, S. (1997). Animal-assisted therapy with hospitalized adolescents. *Journal of Child Adolescent Psychiatry Nursing, 10*(1), 17–24.

Barker, R. T., Knisely, J. S., Barker, S. B., Cobb, R. K., & Schubert, C. M. (2012). Preliminary investigation of employee's dog presence on stress and organizational perceptions. *International Journal of Workplace Health Management, 5*(1), 15–30.

Barker, S. B., & Dawson, K. S. (1998). The effects of animal-assisted therapy on anxiety ratings of hospitalized psychiatric patients. *Psychiatric Services, 49*(6), 797–801. Retrieved from https://www.ncbi.nlm.nih.gov/pubmed/9634160

Barker, S. B., Knisely, J. S., McCain, N. L., & Best, A. M. (2005). Measuring stress and immune response in healthcare professionals following interaction with at therapy dog: A pilot study. *Psychological Reports, 96,* 713–729.

Calcaterra, V., Veggiotti, P., Palestrini, C., Giorgis, V., Raschetti, R., Tumminelli, M., . . . Pelizzo, G. (2015). Post-operative benefits of animal-assisted therapy in pediatric surgery: A randomized study. *PLoS One, 10*(6). https://doi.org/10.1371/journal.pone.0125813

Centers for Disease Control and Prevention. (2017). One Health: Zoonotic Diseases. Retrieved from https://www.cdc.gov/onehealth/basics/zoonotic-diseases.html

Chur-Hansen, A., McArthur, M., Winefield, H., Hanieh, E., & Hazel, S. (2014). Animal-assisted interventions in children's hospitals: A critical review of the literature. *Anthrozoös, 27*(1), 5–18. https://doi.org/10.2752/175303714X13837396326251

Cole, K. M., Gawlinski, A., Steers, N., & Kotlerman, J. (2007). Animal-assisted therapy in patients hospitalized with heart failure. *American Journal of Critical Care, 16*(6), 575–585. Retrieved from https://www.ncbi.nlm.nih.gov/pubmed/17962502

Friedmann, E., Thomas, S. A., & Son, H. (2011). Pets, depression and long-term survival in community living patients following myocardial infarction. *Anthrozoös, 24*(3), 273–285. https://doi.org/10.2752/175303711x13045914865268

Harper, C. M., Dong, Y., Thornhill, T. S., Wright, J., Ready, J., Brick, G. W., & Dyer, G. (2015). Can therapy dogs improve pain and satisfaction after total joint arthroplasty? A randomized controlled trial. *Clinical Orthopaedics and Related Research, 473*(1), 372–379.

Havey, J., Vlasses, F. R., Vlasses, P. H., Ludwig-Beymer, P., & Hackbarth, D. (2014). The effect of animal-assisted therapy on pain medication use after joint replacement. *Anthrozoös, 27*(3), 361–369. https://doi.org/10.2752/175303714x13903827487962

Kaminski, M., Pellino, T., & Wish, J. (2002). Play and pets: The physical and emotional impact of child-life and pet therapy on hospitalized children. *Children's Health Care, 31*(4), 321–335.

Lynch, C. E., Magann, E. F., Barringer, S. N., Ounpraseuth, S. T., Eastham, D. G., Lewis, S. D., & Stowe, Z. N. (2014). Pet therapy program for antepartum high-risk pregnancies: A pilot study. *Journal of Perinatology, 34*(11), 816–818. https://doi.org/10.1038/jp.2014.120

McCracken, K., LaJoie, S., Polis, R., Hertweck, S. P., & Loveless, M. (2016). Impact of therapy dog on patient satisfaction in an outpatient pediatric and adolescent gynecology office. *Journal of Pediatric and Adolescent Gynecology, 29*(2), 195.

Murthy, R., Bearman, G., Brown, S., Bryant, K., Chinn, R., Hewlett, A., . . . Weber, D. J. (2015). Animals in healthcare facilities: Recommendations to minimize potential risks. *Infection Control & Hospital Epidemiology, 36*(05), 495–516.

Nepps, P., Stewart, C. N., & Bruckno, S. R. (2014). Animal-assisted activity: Effects of a complementary intervention program on psychological and physiological variables. *Journal of Evidence-Based Complementary & Alternative Medicine, 19*(3), 211–215. https://doi.org/10.1177/2156587214533570

Sobo, E. J., Eng, B., & Kassity-Krich, N. (2006). Canine visitation (pet) therapy: Pilot data on decreases in child pain perception. *Journal Holistic Nursing, 24*(1), 51–57. https://doi.org/10.1177/0898010105280112

Stufflebeam, D. L. (2007). CIPP evaluation model checklist. The Evaluation Center, Western Michigan University. Retrieved from https://wmich.edu/sites/default/files/attachments/u350/2014/cippchecklist_mar07.pdf

Tsai, C.-C., Friedmann, E., & Thomas, S. A. (2010). The effect of animal-assisted therapy on stress responses in hospitalized children. *Anthrozoös, 23*(3), 245–258. https://doi.org/10.2752/175303710x12750451258977

# Additional Resources

Alliance of Therapy Dogs
PO Box 20227, Cheyenne, WY 82003
www.therapydogs.com

American Veterinary Medical Association
www.avma.org

Canine Companions for Independence
National Headquarters
1-866-CCI-DOGS (224-3647)
PO Box 446, Santa Rosa, CA 95402-0446
www.cci.org

Center for Human–Animal Interaction
PO Box 980710, Richmond, VA 23298
www.chai.vcu.edu

Centers for Disease Control and Prevention
One Health: Zoonotic Diseases
https://www.cdc.gov/onehealth/basics/zoonotic-diseases.html

Fine, A. H. (Ed.). (2015). *Handbook on animal-assisted therapy: Foundations and guidelines for animal-assisted interventions* (4th ed.). London, UK: Academic Press.

Intermountain Therapy Animals
4050 South 2700 East, Salt Lake City, UT 84124
www.therapyanimals.org

Pet Partners
875 124th Ave NE, Suite 101, Bellevue, WA 98005
www.petpartners.org

Society for Healthcare Epidemiology of America
www.shea-online.org

U.S. Department of Justice, Civil Rights Division, Disability Rights Section
*ADA Requirements: Service Animals*
https://www.ada.gov/service_animals_2010.htm

U.S. Department of Justice, Civil Rights Division, Disability Rights Section
*A Guide to Disability Rights Laws*
www.ada.gov/cguide.htm

U.S. Department of Labor
Occupational Information Network, O*NET OnLine
www.onetonline.org

U.S. Office of Personnel Management
www.opm.gov

Therapy Dogs International
88 Bartley Road, Flanders, NJ 07836
www.tdi-dog.org